TWAYNE'S WORLD AUTHORS SERIES

A Survey of the World's Literature

Sylvia E. Bowman, Indiana University

GENERAL EDITOR

SPAIN

Gerald Wade, Vanderbilt University

EDITOR

Alfonso X, El Sabio

(*TWAS 12*)

TWAYNE'S WORLD AUTHORS SERIES (TWAS)

The purpose of TWAS is to survey the major writers —novelists, dramatists, historians, poets, philosophers, and critics—of the nations of the world. Among the national literatures covered are those of Australia, Canada, China, Eastern Europe, France, Germany, Greece, India, Italy, Japan, Latin America, New Zealand, Poland, Russia, Scandinavia, Spain, and the African nations, as well as Hebrew, Yiddish, and Latin Classical literatures. This survey is complemented by Twayne's United States Authors Series and English Authors Series

The intent of each volume in these series is to present a critical-analytical study of the works of the writer; to include biographical and historical material that may be necessary for understanding, appreciation, and critical appraisal of the writer; and to present all material in clear, concise English—but not to vitiate the scholarly content of the work by doing so.

Alfonso X, El Sabio

By JOHN ESTEN KELLER

University of North Carolina

Twayne Publishers, Inc. :: New York

To Laurie and Jack

Preface

In many ways King Alfonso X, known to his people as *El Sabio,* "The Learned," was one of the most important rulers in the Middle Ages, and his reign (1252–84) has been rightly called a kind of thirteenth-century Renaissance. During his rule the arts and sciences flourished in Christian Spain as never before. His code of laws, *Las Siete Partidas,* "The Seven Divisions," is extremely detailed and complete and is the most widely distributed geographically of all legal codes. Its influence, particularly in those American countries and states which were once Spanish possessions, is still felt, and it is, of course, still the foundation of all Spanish law. Alfonso's book entitled *Las Tablas Alfonsinas,* "The Alfonsine Tables" and his world-famous *Lapidarios,* "Lapidaries," to mention only two of his many scientific contributions, enjoyed great acclaim and vogue in Europe until well into the true Renaissance. In a lighter vein, his *Libro de Ajedrez, Dados e Tablas,* "Book of Chess, Dice and Backgammon," was one of the foundation stones of these pastimes and is responsible to no small degree for their development in the Western world. His histories, that of Spain entitled *La Crónica General,* "The General Chronicle," and the incomplete history of the world, *La Grande e General Estoria,* "Great and General History," provide information found nowhere else in medieval books. Students of art, music, literature, folklore, and anthropology prefer his *Cantigas de Santa María,* "Canticles of Holy Mary," for this book with its illuminated miniatures, haunting lyrics, and variegated poetic meters is a truly remarkable blending of the arts.

Such a king, in days when monarchs busied themselves primarily with conquest, war, and diplomacy, inevitably became the focal point of numerous legends. Legends, after all, spring up around the names of all great figures and reveal them to the eye of posterity in unreal and exaggerated colors. Legends feed upon that which is startling, exciting, different, and moving, and though the truth may lie at the root of legend, the truth need not be exact. Two legends in particular revolve around the name of Alfonso the Learned, and neither is flattering to the man or to the monarch. The first, which in all likelihood gained oral currency in the King's own lifetime, is attested first in written form in a late fifteenth-century history and was taken up and perpetuated by subsequent chroniclers. According to this legend, the King once stated: "If I had been with God when He created the world and all that in it is, many mistakes which were made would not have been made." The second legend, hardly more complimentary than the first, was started by a noted historian who wrote: "While he contemplated the heavens and observed the stars, he lost the earth."

The legend, then, of an impractical ruler, of a royal dreamer who charted the paths of the planets, wrote music and verse, spent vast sums of money upon Moorish and Jewish scientists, protected heretical Albigensian troubadours, collected miracles attributed to the Blessed Virgin and squandered the revenues of Castile in an attempt to gain imperial titles, blossomed and survived the centuries, unjustifiably creating a false impression of one of Europe's great kings. For history reveals that Alfonso was actually not an ineffective ruler. He won wars, attempted to organize the judiciary, showed Europe that Spain was to be feared and respected, kept Islam at bay, arranged the proper alliances through treaty and royal marriage, and performed most of the duties one expects of kings. If he made mistakes, if he found himself unable to solve the nation's problems, other kings had made mistakes equally as important and as serious. And if his reign was strife-torn, no Spanish monarch ever ruled a peaceful Spain, and many before Alfonso and after him left kingdoms in worse condition than he.

And yet, behind the most fantastic legends at least some grains of truth are present. Could Alfonso, devout to the point of utter credulity, have expressed the blasphemy ascribed to him in the chronicle? Could a man of his deep intelligence and wisdom have been so blinded by the love of study that he failed markedly to manage his realm? Most probably not. The truth lies in the fact that he was far in advance of the people of his times, and this he must have known quite well. A person oriented as Alfonso was—possibly the only individual in all Europe so oriented—who saw the vast possibilities of scientific research, of planned social order and of royally sponsored cultural pursuits, must have felt extreme frustration in a world which apparently could not or would not accept what he proposed for its improvement. Misunderstood, imposed upon by members of his family who took advantage of his benevolence at every turn, driven into exile by his own son, and constantly hindered by a powerful and resentful nobility, might he not have lashed out with some angrily boastful remark? Indeed, might he not actually have come to believe that his vast knowledge placed him high above other men? Possibly so.

I have dwelt upon the stories concerning King Alfonso's purported vanity and impracticality because they reveal much of the Learned King's life and character and hint at his abilities and his weaknesses. These protests against him provide us with considerable insight into the number and the kind of pressures which seem to have driven him with increasing frequency away from statecraft and into areas of interest in which his true genius could reveal itself. They show us that Alfonso's purpose was the assembling of knowledge from all available sources at his disposal and the dissemination of his information throughout his realm *in Spanish, a language his subjects could understand* rather than in Latin, the usual vehicle of learned writings. Perhaps King Alfonso was at times vain and impractical, but it would be difficult to maintain that these failings characterized his long reign. If he was, we should be thankful, for posterity has gained from his shortcomings.

Volumes have been written, and will doubtless continue to appear, about the Learned King. A definitive study of the scientific works alone, for example, might comprise several tomes. Recently a Spanish historian has devoted over one thousand pages to the life of the monarch. New editions of his works are being published almost every year. The man and his remarkable production, then, are being carefully re-examined and re-evaluated by specialists in various areas of research.

Alfonso X, el Sabio is not a complete biography, nor is it a definitive critical appraisal of the many contributions of this king. It

is designed rather to be a general survey of his life and works—
the first such treatise written in English—and their place in the
unfolding of Spanish culture in the Middle Ages. This study is
based upon sound and up-to-date books, monographs, and articles
and upon certain opinions of my own which have been developed
after reading the extant Alfonsine documents. Chapter 1 treats
the structure of society in Alfonso's times and offers a very brief
history of Spain before his rule; Chapter 2 presents a résumé
of Alfonso's life and the major events that took place while he
lived; Chapter 3 is a general survey of Spanish letters prior to
and contemporary with Alfonso X; Chapter 4 is a study of the
first literary text of Alfonso, while he was still a prince, for *Calila
e Digna* was completed before he ascended the throne; Chapter
5 studies the threefold media—artistic, musical, and poetic—of
the *Cantigas de Santa María;* Chapter 6 treats the *Cantigas Profanas;* Chapter 7 discusses the legalistic works with the emphasis
on the *Siete Partidas;* Chapter 8 surveys the scientific works; and
Chapter 9 is devoted to the historical works.

JOHN ESTEN KELLER

Chapel Hill, North Carolina

I wish to express my gratitude to the Ecclesiastical Authorities
of the library at the Monastery of San Lorenzo del Escorial in
Spain for permission to have photographed the rare miniatures
of the *Cantigas de Santa María,* and to Sr. Tomas Magallón, official photographer of the Biblioteca Nacional in Madrid, for his
patience and skill in taking these pictures; also to the Biblioteca
Nazionale of Florence for permission to photograph the manuscript of the *Cantigas* among its holdings.

Special thanks is also given to the Research Fund of the University of North Carolina for grants used in the collecting, preparation, and typing of the materials used in this book. The help given
me by Dr. Louise M. Hall and Mrs. Alan B. MacIntyre of the
Library of the University of North Carolina in locating rare books
and monographs has been invaluable to me, and I thank them
for it.

Acknowledgment is made to the Clarendon Press, Oxford, for
its kind permission to quote from Dr. Evelyn S. Proctor's *Alfonso
X, Patron of Literature and Learning* (Oxford, 1951) and to *Gems*

and Gemology, which allowed me to quote copiously from an article of mine published there (Winter, 1957–58).

The many scholarly articles, monographs, and books which have contributed to this work cannot all be mentioned here, nor can the titles of the many journals which published these contributions, but mention of many of these will be found in the Bibliography of this book.

Last, but not least, I give special thanks to Dr. William C. McCrary of the Department of Romance Languages of the University of North Carolina for his kindness in reading the manuscript of this book and for his careful and detailed criticism of it and his suggestions for its improvement.

Chronology

409 End of Roman rule in Spain: the Peninsula is overrun by Alans, Suevi, and Vandals.

456 After four decades of strife the Visigoths rule in Spain.

654 Hispano-Roman and Visigothic laws fused in *Forum Judicum*.

711 Islamic invasion led by Tarik: Fall of Kingdom of the Visigoths.

718 Battle of Covadonga, a Christian victory: Beginning of the Reconquest by the Christians.

778 Charlemagne invades Spain: French disaster at the Pass of Roncesvalles.

791 Oviedo made capital of Asturias.

914 León established as capital of León.

c. 950 County of Castile wins independence from León.

1031 Caliphate of Cordova, founded in 928, collapses: Andalusia breaks up into *taifas*, "petty kingdoms."

1035 Castile and Aragon become Kingdoms.

1085 Capture of Toledo by Alfonso VI of Castile and León.

1086– The Almoravides reunite Andalusia.
1090

1099 Death of the Cid.

1130 Alfonso VII of Castile establishes school of translators in Toledo.

1146 Almohades invade Andalusia.

1212 Christians defeat Moslems decisively at Las Navas de Tolosa.

1221 Birth of Alfonso, first son of Ferdinand III and Beatriz of Suabia.

1230 Reunion of Castile and León.

1236 Ferdinand III takes Cordova from Moors.

1244 Marriage of Alfonso to Violante, daughter of James of Aragon.

1248 Prince Alfonso takes Murcia and concludes peace with Moors: Ferdinand and Prince Alfonso capture Seville.

1251 Prince Alfonso has Arabic classic translated as *Calila e Digna*.

1252 May 30: Death of Ferdinand III. May 31: Coronation of Alfonso X. Birth of Prince Sancho, who will rule as Sancho IV.

1254 Betrothal of Alfonso's half-sister to English prince who will rule as Edward I.

1255 *Fuero Real* finished under Alfonso's patronage. Alfonso's brother Enrique leads revolt.

1256– Alfonso tries to gain title of Emperor of Holy Roman Em-
1272 pire.

1257 Completion of the first one hundred of *Cantigas de Santa María*.

1259 Fall of Jerez de la Frontera: Revolt of Enrique quelled.

1262– Astronomical observations conducted by Alfonso at Toledo.
1272

1264 Moorish Andalusia in revolt: Alfonso quells it.

1265 Cadiz taken from the Moors: Granada becomes vassal state next year.

1268 Alfonso frees Portugal from vassalage to Spain.

1269 Revolt of Alfonso's brother Felipe.

1270 *Crónica General* begun.

1272– Revolt of the nobles.
1274

1275 Alfonso meets Gregory X at Beaucaire. Death of Prince Ferdinand, heir apparent: Prince Sancho claims throne.

1276 *Espéculo de las Leyes* completed.

1279 Definitive edition of *Cantigas de Santa María* completed.

1280 First part of *Grand e General Estoria* finished.

1282 Alfonso deposed by Prince Sancho and the nobles: Alfonso flees to Seville and enlists help of Moroccan Moors.

1283 Completion of *Libro de Ajedrez, Dados y Tablas*.

1284 April 4: Alfonso X dies in Seville.

CHAPTER 1

The Medieval Spains

I *The Structure of Society*

WHEN Alfonso X ascended the throne in 1252 he assessed and understood the problems and the advantages laid out before him. The advantages certainly were many, and no monarch in Europe had a right to higher hopes and greater expectations. His father, Ferdinand III, later canonized as St. Ferdinand for his wars against the infidel, had left Castile and Leon strong and respected. Ferdinand's renown was phenomenal, and Alfonso himself was highly regarded abroad, as well as in Spain. The royal house of Castile, by marriage or actual kinship, was linked with important sovereigns in the West. Ferdinand had married a German princess, Beatriz of Suabia, granddaughter of Frederick Barbarossa; Alfonso's brother, Felipe, would marry Cristina of Norway, daughter of Haakon IV; Fadrique, another brother, was to wed Catalina, daughter of Nicephoro Angelo, Despot of Rumania; royal ties existed between Castile and Portugal; Edward I of England would make Alfonso's half-sister, Leonor, Queen of England, adding another Spanish princess to the British line; Louis IX was Alfonso's second cousin; King Baldwin of Constantinople married Alfonso's first cousin, María de Brena; another cousin, Vladislao III, was King of Bohemia; still another cousin ruled in Sicily; of more importance, perhaps, was an uncle, James of Aragon, whose daughter by Violante, sister of King Bela IV of Hungary, Alfonso married in 1244. The Castilian Monarch must have derived a deep sense of security from such connections. And at the beginning of his reign, at least, Pope Innocent IV considered him important and gave him his support.[1]

Furthermore, the Moors, to all intents and purposes had been weakened beyond any hope of true recovery. Only Granada, the last of their kingdoms in the Peninsula, had survived, and although it would continue as a kingdom for some two centuries, its king was a vassal of Castile. Granada paid tribute, and though she was never truly loyal, and at times even harbored the enemies of the crown, she never posed a serious threat to the Spanish hegemony. Even the Moors in Africa had ceased to be an actual threat, and no great invasions from that quarter were envisaged or feared by Alfonso as he took over the reins of government. So much for the advantages and happy prospects.

Nevertheless, the problems the new king faced, from the very first, were serious. Alfonso's great knowledge of history must have prepared him for the difficulties to come, even though this knowledge could not offer the necessary solution. All Spanish kings before Alfonso's time had faced this dilemma, and after his reign few monarchs would be free of it. This problem lay in the aristocrats and the great powers they possessed. The nobility, by Spanish law, could not be taxed. Neither could the Church, nor the great military orders, Alcántara, Santiago and Calatrava, which owed their allegiance to the Pope. Only the towns and the common people bore the brunt of taxation, and even before Alfonso's rule their contribution had not sufficed to support the monarchy. What had maintained it was the revenue brought in from wars against the Moors, from booty and pillage, from tribute and extortion, and from territories wrested from the enemy. Both the crown and the nobility had profited. Now with all but the last of the Moorish kingdoms defeated, occupied and distributed among the demanding nobles, this source of income had come to an end. The nobles grew understandably restive. For some five hundred years, since the beginnings of the Reconquest at the Battle of Covadonga when Spaniards first defeated a force of the Moorish conqueror, the nobility had made a profession of war and a business out of the spoils of war. A way of life, centuries old, was drawing to a close. Since they had provided the crown with armies to fight the Moslems, and since they had grown wealthy in pursuits certainly not pacific, they found it difficult to settle into the ways of peace and to abide by the wishes of a king who seemed all too interested in building a world that would eventually rob them of power. They became, for Alfonso X, what they had become in the past from time to time to other kings: a constant threat. Revolts were frequent

[22]

and in the end the restless nobility deposed their ruler and placed his rebellious son upon the throne.

From the beginnings of the Reconquest, Spanish kings had seen the importance of the burghers who had to pay the taxes. To offset the power of the nobles, sovereigns had granted *fueros,* or rights and privileges to towns, many of which had been founded as mere frontier outposts in or near Moorish territory. These towns had the authority for self-government, the right to assess taxes upon themselves and—predictably—as time went on, they demanded and received representation. Here were the beginnings of a middle class. Here, too, could be seen the emergence of a balance of power, for the king granted the towns representation in the Cortes or early parliaments. And the towns, made up of a middle class with rights and privileges, felt themselves to be closely associated with the national welfare, and therefore, a very important part of the nation. Kings who were skilful at statecraft knew how to play town against nobility. All this Alfonso must have noted carefully and planned to cope with.

II *The Backgrounds of History: Christian Spain*

Scholar that he was, Alfonso had studied rigorously the flow of history in the Iberian Peninsula. He was fiercely proud of the land he would rule and of its ancient and venerable heritage. First of all was the Roman birthright which he recognized as of great pertinence to his people. But this inheritance was shared by France and Italy and even Britain and the Germanies. After all, some thousand years of Roman rule in Europe had produced a way of life and culture that stretched unbroken from the Roman walls in Britain to the gates of Parthia. The Roman genealogy, then, was not unique to Spain. Then there was the Visigothic background. All Spaniards looked with warm sentiments to the Gothic kings of old, but Alfonso knew that these Germanic invaders had entered the Peninsula more than half-Romanized, that their records and other writings had been set down in Latin, and that Spain's debt to them lay primarily in the infusion of a new and vigorous blood and in a line of monarchs whose descendants would rule Spain for centuries to come. He also knew that the cultural contributions of the Visigoths had been somewhat meager and that the greatest figures among them were churchmen. Spain could hardly be considered a national entity during the years of Visigothic rule, not even toward the end, when Roderick, the last king, lost his realm to the Moslem invaders from Africa.[2]

Truly national entity, Alfonso knew, began when a few Hispano-Visigothic nobles and churchmen slipped through the Moorish armies and escaped into the vastnesses of the Cantabrian Mountains of the Asturias. Led by Pelayo, who seems to have been an important official at the Toledan court of Roderick, these refugees laid the foundations of the Spanish nation. Only seven years after the invasion and seizure of Spain by the Moslems led by Tarik, Pelayo and his men defeated—for the first time—a Moslem force at Covadonga in 718 and by so doing initiated the Reconquest. Such were the origins of Castile and Leon, and these beginnings were owed—though few would have admitted it—to the invader himself. Without the Moorish conquest of Spain, that small group of determined men would not have joined together and fought to keep their identity; and without their struggle, there would have been no Reconquest and possibly no nation like the Spain we know today. King Roderick, then, although he died in battle on the banks of the Guadalete River near Jerez de la Frontera, did not die in vain, for his loss of Spain to the Moslems actually led to the birth of the new and revitalized Spain beyond the reach of the Moors in Asturias.

Alfonso X, to be sure, realized, as we do today, that the invasion from Africa, which brought an utterly foreign enemy into Spain, of completely different culture, civilization, faith and philosophy, was not the catastrophe it had appeared to be to the Christians who were overthrown. With the subsequent cultural and racial mingling of Christians and Moslems a new individualism and a new identity had come to Spain. It was this necessary deviation from the Western way of life that made the Spain Alfonso was to rule a quasi-oriental, quasi-occidental domain. Probably few of Alfonso's contemporaries understood this as well as he: certainly none made such a concentrated effort to capitalize upon this Eastern inheritance.

Spain in the thirteenth century was still a divided land: the

North, the central area almost entirely, and some sectors of the South were Christian and maintained firm ties with the main currents of European civilization. The South, Andalusia, the cradle and center of Moorish civilization, was Moslem and looked toward Africa and the rest of Islam. And so North and South, Christian and Moor, coexisted geographically and culturally: neither was the Christian entirely "Western," nor the Moslem wholly "Eastern." Each had been greatly altered by his neighbor, and each had gained by the change. The history of Christian Spain from the middle of the eighth century is by necessity implicated in the history of Moslem Spain; thus one cannot be viewed without the other.

With the victory at Covadonga, then, as Alfonso recognized, medieval Spanish history acquired a new direction and personality. Asturias, with its capital at Oviedo, became the seat of Iberian Christendom, and from there, despite limited manpower, the *Reconquista* emanated. From time to time, the struggling Asturians received aid from Europeans across the Pyrenees. Charlemagne had tried to defeat the Moslem armies at Saragossa: this attempt occasioned the disaster at the Pass of Roncesvalles when his armies crossed into France on their homeward journey. The French emperor's son, Louis, was more successful; he seized Barcelona from the Moors in 801 and removed Catalonia from Islamic domination. By 950 the County of Castile had won its freedom from León, which itself had emerged as a kingdom from the little monarchy of Asturias, and in 987 the Catalonians won their freedom from France, although they never cut their ties with that important country and remained as much French as Spanish. The Christians were indeed on the move. Thus, León, the capital of the Kingdom of León, was built beyond the protection of the Cantabrian Mountains and within reach of Islamic armies. Soon Castile, which in 950 separated from León to form a county, with Burgos as its capital, initiated its own contribution to the Reconquest.

Alfonso had reason to be proud of Castile. Founded on castle fortresses, from which it got its name, almost constantly at war in those early years with the Moslem foe, it prospered and grew powerful with the strength frontier countries must develop to survive. Castile had little time to think of tradition and the past, which the more secure León could do. Castile lived in the dangerous present and faced a perilous future. Even the laws promulgated in settled and more civilized León meant little to people who lived in the actual shadow of war. Therefore Castilians made their own laws to fit the situations and emergencies that presented themselves. Alfonso was also proud of his people's language, and by using it instead of Latin, even in technical areas like jurisprudence and diplomacy, he turned it into the clear and logical literary vehicle it became in his reign.

In 1035 the County of Castile, founded by Fernán González a century before, became officially a kingdom ruled by Ferdinand I who reigned until 1065. It was this king who defeated León in war and made Castile the dominant kingdom. His victory came only four years after the Caliphate of Cordova fell and was fragmented into dozens of *taifas* or petty kingdoms, leaving Spanish Islam without a political center. The Reconquest would soon roll unstopped into Andalusia. Not even the terrible defeat of the Christians at Alarcos in 1195 when King Alfonso VIII, with no allies, was defeated by Moorish forces, could destroy the Christian impetus. By 1212, this time with the allied armies of Navarre, Aragon, and León to support his Castilian troops, Alfonso VIII gave what may be regarded as the coup de grâce to Spanish Islam. This sovereign was the grandfather of Alfonso X, and the Battle of Las Navas de Tolosa, as this signal victory was called, had occurred only some forty years before the Learned King's birth.

The next forty years after Las Navas saw Ferdinand, Alfonso's own father, take up the crusade against the Moor, and to Ferdinand it had indeed been a crusade, a war to destroy a pagan enemy and plant the cross in infidel lands. Ferdinand turned the Great Mosque of Cordova into a Christian cathedral, attacked the enemy in Africa, captured Seville and other important Moorish holdings, and would have subdued Granada itself had death not overtaken him. Alfonso lived through much of this latter part of his father's crusade, and even helped personally in the siege and capture of Seville; and just prior to this triumph he had led the Spanish forces that captured Murcia.

[26]

III   *Moorish Spain*

Alfonso's knowledge of the history of Spanish Islam was no less thorough than his grasp of Christian development. He had at his disposal not only the chronicles of his own people, but also histories written by the Moslems and translated for his convenience. Moslem history was as colorful as its Christian counterpart. The Moors first had come to Spain, he knew, in the year 711 when a Berber leader in the pay of Arab masters led some 20,000 troops across the Strait of Gibraltar.[3] This man was Tarik, and the rock at which he landed his troops was called Gebel-Tarik or "Tarik's Rock." His sweep up the entire Peninsula had been phenomenally swift, and within a year the Crescent fluttered from the Mediterranean to the Pyrenees. Only in the valleys of the Asturias did Christians under Pelayo maintain a shaky independence. Islam, history revealed, by and large, had not been a harsh master. Christians who lived under her sway were allowed to keep their faith and to practice it. They were called by their conquerors Mozarabs, that is, "Those-who-lived-as-Arabs," or the "Almost-Arabs." Cut off from their Christian compatriots in Europe, they learned Arabic, often intermarried with Moslems, dressed in the eastern fashion, and enjoyed a cultural level higher than their kinsmen beyond the Moorish frontier.

Alfonso had read of Moorish Cordova, known as the "Pearl of the West" and had seen with his own eyes its fading glories. If the 50,000 palaces and mansions, the 900 public baths, the 700 mosques, and the great library with its 400,000 volumes no longer existed, or were only the exaggerated accounts of Moorish historians, Alfonso knew that they could have existed. Certainly much of the eastern wisdom contained in those volumes was extant and ready for the translators Alfonso employed to render them into his own language. Cordova undoubtedly remained a great treasure house of Spain's Islamic past.

The chroniclers, both Moorish and Christian, related the gradual softening and weakening of the original invaders and told of their retreat before the advances of their Spanish enemies. The fierce Almorávides, "Those-vowed-to-God," truly fanatic and newly converted zealots of Islam, entered Spain to save it from the Christian Reconquest and stayed on to keep it for themselves. The leader of these warrior-monks from Marrakesh, Yuçuf, left his son, Ali, to rule Andalusia (1106–43), and the persecution of Christians began with fearful severity. Thousands of the Christian Mozarabs fled northward, thousands more were sold as slaves into Barbary, and still other thousands were put to the sword. Out of this period of martyrdom and bloodletting, a renewed hatred and terror of the Moslem was born, but at the same time came a familiarity with the cultural advantages of Moorish civilization through the Mozarabs who reached the Christian kingdoms bringing much of that culture with them.

In due time, Alfonso knew, the Almorávides had succumbed to Andalusia's luxurious spell, and like their conquered predecessors, exchanged their puritanical piety for pleasure and wealth. As a result, they were unable to hold back the ever encroaching armies of the Reconquest, and in panic they begged aid from Moslem sovereigns in Africa. This time it was the newly converted Berber tribes from the Atlas Mountains who called themselves the Almohades, "The Unitarians." Their purpose, like that of the Almorávides themselves, aside from that of seizing a rich and fertile land, was the purification of Spanish Islam. By 1150 these proponents of militant Islam were in possession of most of Andalusia. Their cruelty to their enemies sent additional thousands of Christians across the frontier. This second persecution must have convinced Castile that so long as Moors occupied any part of Spain, others would come out of Africa to help their compatriots and often subsequently to conquer them. With this in mind, Alfonso VIII challenged Sultan Yacub, and Yacub accepted the challenge, appearing in 1195 at Alarcos, not far from Badajoz with a mighty army. As we have seen, Alarcos was a disaster and a tragedy for Spanish arms. So decisive and terrible was the Moorish victory that all Spain trembled and made ready for a revival of the days of Tarik. The Moslem tide reached as far inland as Madrid and might well have been carried even further had not Yacub's stronger interests at home called him back to Morocco. The mistake he made in leaving a chastened but not a conquered Spain was soon evident. For, as Alfonso had learned from the Spanish chronicles and even from the accounts of people who had lived through the events, the Spains—Castile, León,

Navarre, and Aragon—had united and given that already mentioned coup de grâce to the Moors at Las Navas de Tolosa. After that most decisive of Christian victories the threat of significant Moslem incursions ended.

As a boy of fifteen Alfonso had rejoiced at his father's conquest of Cordova in 1236; he rejoiced again two years later when his uncle, James of Aragon, wrested Valencia and the Balearic Islands from the Moslems. In 1248 his delight was personal, for in that year he commanded the armies that captured Murcia and assisted his father in the siege and storming of Seville. In the latter he saw firsthand the wonders of a Moorish capital, and in the fertile plain surrounding the city was able to observe the remarkable advances in agriculture and particularly in irrigation. Only the Kingdom of Granada remained between Christendom and total victory.

With the Reconquest all but completed, Alfonso was able to turn enthusiastically to the study of Moorish culture and science. This newly won Moslem world of Andalusia would continue to be the channel through which eastern learning would enter the West, but under Alfonso it would be a deeper and broader channel. He wisely saw that Spain's heritage from the Moors was as Spanish as the heritage handed down to his people from their Roman and Visigothic ancestors. As subsequent chapters will show, he profited greatly by this discovery and saw to it that great portions of this inheritance from the East were translated into his nation's language.

CHAPTER 2

Alfonso X, the Man and the King

ALFONSO, Prince of Castile, heir to the double throne of León and Castile, was born on Tuesday, November 23, 1221 and, fittingly enough, in the "Imperial City" of Toledo where much of his later studies would take place.[1] Little is known of his early years, for contemporary chronicles devote no space to that period. An occasional privilege or royal grant, however, provides brief insights into his childhood and youth. One of these privileges was granted by Alfonso's father, Ferdinand III to the child's *nodriza* "wet nurse," a noble lady named Urraca Pérez, wife of Don García Alvarez of Toledo. The privileges granted to her and her husband the township of Portillo, "For the many services which you have done and are doing for me in the rearing of my first-born son Alfonso." As this was issued in the prince's tenth year, we know that he was still under the care of this couple.

A later privilege, granted this time by Alfonso himself after he had become king, tells us that his *ayo* "tutor" was none other than the faithful supporter of the royal house since the times of Alfonso VIII, Alfonso's grandfather. This gentleman was Don Garci Fernández, a man well-fitted to rear a prince and train him in the ways of chivalry, warfare, and statecraft. In this privilege which grants him certain lands we read: ". . . because Don Garci Fernández and his wife Doña Mayor Arias reared me and did me many services, and especially because they brought me up in Villaldemiro and in Celada." [2] The prince grew up in the rural atmosphere of these remote places and in others belonging to his *ayo*, and probably saw a great deal more of his royal servitors than of his parents, Queen Beatriz and King Ferdinand. From legal treatises and books intended as guides for the rearing of royal children we learn that this was the custom. Cities, crowded and unsanitary and filled with undesirables, were no place for the important offspring of monarchs.

The authority on the life of Alfonso, the historian Ballesteros,[3] believes that among the holdings of the prince's tutor was the village of Orense in Galicia, home of the troubadours, and that there the boy heard and fell in love with the soft, sweet speech used in the thirteenth century, indeed for several centuries to come, as the vehicle for nearly all the lyric poetry composed and written in Spain. Galician was a dialect of Portuguese, and its soft sibilant tongue intrigued the prince who wrote in it prolifically. In Galicia, also, he may have fallen under the influence of the many legends and superstitions of a people whose ancestry went back to the Celtic invaders of antiquity. To this day not even the Irish lean more toward the world of fairies and elves than do the Gallegos. The mark of that cloudy land of wooded mountains and mystery may have had a greater effect upon Alfonso than anyone realizes.

Another effect, certainly a strong one, too, to judge by some of the prince's and later the king's poetic compositions known as *cantigas de escarnio* "songs of mockery," must have been produced by his stay in the army camps and the rough military life to which he was exposed. A prince who someday would rule Spain of necessity had to learn soldiery, and such knowledge could not come from books alone. Therefore the king saw to it that Alfonso lived and traveled with the army. If he learned more than military tactics, if he associated with rough mercenaries from abroad, with Moorish troops who fought for the king who would pay the highest wage, with camp followers and dancing girls and troubadours and all the flotsam and jetsam that accompanied armies on the march or attached themselves to encampments, the king could only regret it. And this, too, was an important part of the formative years of Alfonso.

Almost certainly the king arranged to have the best teachers, scientists, and legal experts in attendance upon his first-born son. Everything points to this. The prince became a voracious reader, a renowned student of history, a young man eager to learn the science of astronomy and the disciplines of astrology and the science of the influence of stones upon human life, which in those days were studied along with the exact sciences. While still a prince he had made a revision of certain astronomical tables that charted the movements of the planets according to the famous Cordovan astronomer, al-Zarqali. Alfonso, in this revision, corrected and verified the findings of the Moor and made astrological observations in Toledo a little later, after he had become king. These *Alfonsine Tables*, about which more will be said shortly, enjoyed great repute in the course of the Middle Ages, and even in the Renaissance.

The law interested the prince, too, and he made a beginning at the legal reforms in his work on the *Fuero Real*, "Royal Codex of Laws," and the *Leyes del Estado*, "Laws of the State," which would result in the *Siete Partidas*, "Seven Divisions of Law." Of great interest to him, also, was literature, and as one might surmise, the writings of the East, imported into Spain by the Moors, attracted him. A year before his coronation he had caused a famous Arabic collection of tales and philosophical tracts to be translated into Spanish as *El Libro de Calila e Digna*, "Book of Calila and Digna," thereby becoming the first to sponsor such a book in a western vernacular tongue. Nor did he overlook pictorial art or music, and a study of the books he commanded to be written will provide some of the best and most detailed insights we have into medieval painting and illumination.

The prince's military and diplomatic training bore fruit when his father placed him at the head of the army which captured Murcia from the Moors. There he not only skilfully laid siege to the city in 1247 and reduced its defenses, but even concluded the treaty of peace with the defeated inhabitants. And a year later in the capture of Seville he led the Spanish troops which took Triana, the suburb of Seville across the Guadalquivir River.[4]

Alfonso married Violante, daughter of James of Aragon and Violante of Hungary, in 1244 when he was twenty-three. She was to bear him six sons—Fernando, Sancho, Pedro, Juan, Jaime, Enrique; and four daughters, Berenguela, Isabel, Leonor and Violante; and she was to be a devoted mother but, in later years, would turn upon her husband. If she made any public or private objections to his two illegitimate children, no mention is made of this by the chroniclers. One of these, the son known as "Alfonso el Niño," made no great mark; but the daughter, Beatriz, whose mother, Doña Mayor Guillén, was the wife of a Spanish grandee, would one day marry the King of Portugal.

To return momentarily to the fall of Seville and the period immediately following the Spanish victory, it should be mentioned that Murcia, barely conquered and given a peace treaty by the Prince, revolted, and Alfonso had to conquer it a second time. Without the support of his young cousin, Alfonso of Aragon, he took the city and this time arranged to prevent further discord there. For two and a half years he ruled Murcia himself, and during this period replaced the rebellious Moorish population with loyal Christian Spaniards. From this he apparently learned an important lesson, for no sooner had he returned to Seville, than he advised his father, who was still there, not to go back to Castile until the Moorish population could be driven out and replaced by Christians. The King agreed, and the repopulation of the city was started.

King Ferdinand's plans included the building of a great navy, one capable of carrying the might of Spain to the shores of Africa. Granada, too, might have enjoyed only a short hegemony had the great king lived, but this was not to be. King Ferdinand died in Seville of an unidentified ailment on May 30, 1252. With him an era ended. With the coronation of his son, Alfonso, an era began. When the thirty-one-year-old Alfonso was crowned in 1252, his realm covered most of the map of Spain. Portugal, Aragon, Catalonia, which belonged to Aragon, and the tributary Kingdom of Granada formed the parts not under his rule. Ferdinand, on his deathbed, had said to his son: "Sir, I bequeath you all the land which the Moors had taken from King Roderick of Spain; and in your power it all remains, part of it conquered, part paying tribute. If you learn how to keep it in the state I bequeath to you, you are a king as good as I; and if you gain more by your own efforts, you are better than I; and if you lose any of it, you are not as good as I." [5] Alfonso loved and respected his father. No one can doubt that he began his reign determined to live up to the heritage placed in his hands.

We must pass rapidly over the first years of the new king's reign. From the beginning he proved to be more lenient than Ferdinand, and this soon brought him to grief. He allowed the

King of Granada to pay less tribute; he was far too generous and free-handed with the nobility; he debased the coinage, as kings before him had done, and in so doing he enraged the populace. But he managed to fill the lands left empty by the Moors, who had departed Spain forever, by granting them to various nobles, kinsmen, church officials and friends. He passed sumptuary laws in an effort to stifle the envy felt by the poor for the rich, and he went so far as to stipulate even the number of inches of velvet that should be worn and the amount of silver and gold that might be used on saddles and bridles; furthermore, sumptuary laws on food and drink were also passed. He outlawed price-fixing; he forbade the contamination of streams from factory wastes; he insisted upon the segregation of Moors and Jews from the Gentiles in Christian cities; he warred with Portugal and won the rich region of Algarbe for Spain, mindful, no doubt, of Ferdinand's admonition about adding to the realm; he insisted upon the rights and privileges of students, whom he regarded as important to the nation; he invaded Gascony, claiming it on the grounds that it had belonged to his great-aunt; but when Henry III of England, whose land it was, offered to have his son Edward marry Alfonso's half-sister Leonor, the Castilian monarch agreed and gave up his claims to Gascony. This took place in 1254. The next year saw the revolt of Alfonso's brother, Enrique, and Alfonso's success in expelling the prince from the kingdom. He married his illegitimate daughter Beatriz to Alfonso of Portugal and returned Algarbe to the Portuguese, much to the displeasure of his nobles.

The years from 1256 to 1272 were interrupted by Alfonso's efforts to gain the title of Emperor of the Holy Roman Empire made vacant by the death of William of Holland. Alfonso claimed rights to the title through his mother, Beatriz of Suabia, and set about to realize his claim. But Pope Alexander IV refused his blessing, since the house of Suabia had long been an enemy of the Papacy. Nor would Urban IV or Clement IV, as each received the Crown of St. Peter, recognize Alfonso's claims. Pope Gregory X went even further: he wrote to Alfonso and told him to withdraw his claims, and to the electors, directing them to declare null and void all present claims so as to elect a candidate who must be one of the German princes; but not one of the house of Suabia, as that house had aided the Guelphs in former times against the Papacy.

When Rudolph, Count of Hapsburg, was elected to the title with the approval of Pope Gregory, Alfonso decided to go to war. He would have as allies a number of Italian princes, notably those of Lombardy and Pisa. But before hostilities actually began, Gregory asked Alfonso to meet him at Beaucaire in France to discuss the entire matter. Alfonso went, leaving the reins of government in the hands of his first-born son, Prince Ferdinand, known as Fernando de la Cerda. This young man was a prince of great promise and the pride of his father's life. He was eighteen at the time of the meeting in Beaucaire. The conference with Gregory was an utter contretemps. Not only did the Pope deny all of Alfonso's rights to the title of Emperor: he did more, blasting the Castilian's aspirations to the Duchy of Suabia; worse still, he refused to approve the marriage of Alfonso's grandson—this youth was the son of Fernando de la Cerda and Blanche of France—to the heir apparent of Navarre. The year was 1275.

Alfonso went back to Castile, still unwilling to admit defeat, although by now his nobles were in open opposition to his imperial aspirations on the grounds that the expenses involved were bankrupting the realm. Pope Gregory finally solved the problem with a threat and a consolation. If Alfonso did not desist, he would suffer excommunication, a thing the pious Alfonso would never face. If he accepted the Pope's decision, Castile could have one-tenth of the ecclesiastical income of Spain for use in the wars against the Moors.

During the years of Alfonso's difficulties with popes and imperial electors other problems arose at home. The Moors of Andalusia and Murcia, aided by Granada and the Moorish king of Morocco, had revolted in 1262 and were raiding far and wide. But disagreement among them led to withdrawal from the war and even desertion to the Christians on the part of some. Alfonso won the war with little difficulty, but a series of similar outbreaks followed. While Alfonso was away and busy with the matter of the imperial title, Fernando de la Cerda carried on the war in Andalusia. During one of the more pressing irruptions of Moorish revolt, Fernando de la Cerda fell ill on the way to Andalusia. He died on the twenty-fifth of July, 1275 and thereby precipitated a series of events ultimately bringing about the end of Alfonso's rule. For as soon as word of his brother's death reached Sancho, the king's second son, this young man claimed to be the heir apparent, thereby displacing the son of Fernando. Such was the state of affairs when the king returned.

If Alfonso hoped that the rebellions were at an end, he was sorely disappointed. The kingdom still bore the effects of the rebellion of his brother, Enrique. The Moors, whose culture and civilization he had always envied, had turned upon him. Lastly, his own son had become the most important and dangerous rebel of all. When this son, Sancho, asked his father to consider him as heir rather than the son of Fernando de la Cerda, the king summoned the nobles to discuss the matter. At the meeting, which was held in Segovia, Alfonso asked them to consider Sancho as his heir. Fearful of what might happen to her grandchildren at the hands of Sancho, Queen Violante and her daughter-in-law, Blanche, fled with the children to Aragon where they sought the protection of the new king, James's son, Pedro. But Sancho persuaded Pedro to imprison the children, lest they be brought back to Castile by those who opposed him. Alfonso seemed to approve of what Sancho was doing and, indeed, did not oppose him but as time went on, perhaps overcome with remorse at what he had allowed to happen to his grandson, the legal heir of Fernando de la Cerda, he tried to persuade Sancho to consider the child's case. Sancho's answer to this was a vigorous "no," and a plot to dethrone his own father. He persuaded his younger brothers, Pedro and Juan, to join him, as well as a large contingent of noblemen. Juan went to León and turned the Leónese against his father; Sancho persuaded the Castilians; the King of Portugal joined the rebels; and the King of Aragon promised his aid if it were required. And Queen Violante herself turned against her husband, siding with Sancho, who almost immediately began to perform many of the duties of royalty.

Abandoned by his immediate family, turned against by his people, all but friendless, Alfonso fled to the safety of the one city that would support him. Seville, he knew, had not abandoned him. From that stronghold he looked about for allies, and at last in extreme desperation did what he had berated others for having done. He enlisted the help of a Moorish king in Morocco, Aben-

Yuzaf. The Moor came with a considerable army, but Sancho, aided by the Moorish king of Granada, was too much for them. He drove Alfonso behind the walls of Seville and sent Aben-Yuzaf in retreat to Africa.

Sancho's difficulties, however, were not at an end. Pope Martin V, enraged at the revolt Sancho was leading against the established government in Spain, excommunicated the prince and urged the French and English to attack him. His two brothers, Pedro and Juan, now deserted him and gave their support again to their father. Beatriz of Portugal, Alfonso's bastard daughter, went to his assistance and later tried to bring about peace between father and son. But on April 24, 1284 reconciliation was no longer necessary. Alfonso, weakened by care, old age, and illness, died. In due time his rebellious son ascended the throne as Sancho IV to be dubbed by his people Sancho el Bravo, that is, "Sancho the Fierce."

So ended the life of the Learned King, a man who had advanced the cause of culture and learning, not only in Spain but even far beyond its borders. The attempts he made, far from being fruitless, greatly enhanced the progress of letters and the arts and sciences. If his contemporaries failed to give his work the praise it deserved, later ages did and will continue to do so. Perhaps Don Juan Ríos Sarmiento in his study of the Learned King best sums up Alfonso's glory and his tragedy. "He was, then, a man whom we can call universal in time and in space. This alone would be sufficient to make him incompatible with the people he governed, who did not know how to appreciate the light which Don Alfonso brought into what is known as the thirteenth-century Renaissance." [6]

Dreamer or not, Alfonso el Sabio is now remembered with reverence, when his detractors and enemies have sunken into darkest oblivion.

CHAPTER 3

Alfonso X, Patron of Arts and Letters

ALFONSO'S interests in arts and letters began while he was
still a prince, and perhaps even while he was still a child. His
concern with the sciences, the law, and history paralleled his
purely literary activities and may have even anticipated them.
For any one interested in the various areas of literature and
learning, contemporary archives could have furnished excellent
backgrounds. Alfonso's father, King Ferdinand, had long been a
sponsor of knowledge, and the royal library must have been ex-
tensive; in addition, there were cathedral and monastic library
holdings of considerable size, and all these would have been at
the royal prince's disposal.[1] Latin literature, both classical and
ecclesiastical, surely was available. Moreover, court troubadours
and minstrels, as well as the many less elegant itinerant members of this profession, were ever on the scene with songs, the
recitation of epic poems and stories of adventure;[2] Moorish and
Jewish professional storytellers wended their way from Andalusia
across all Spain and into Europe beyond the Pyrenees; while
down from Germany, England and France, and even from farther
afield, came hordes of pilgrims en route to the Tomb of St. James
at Compostela in Galicia.[3] If Alfonso spent time in Galicia, that
land of troubadours, as is believed, then he must have seen the
pilgrim throngs as well as the droves of beggars, jugglers, singers
and dancers, story-tellers, and rogues that followed the pilgrims
to entertain or prey upon them.

   In Galicia, too, he would have heard the troubadours themselves as they poured out their sweet and sad songs of love. There
would also have been the lewd and rough ditties shouted by soldiers and travelers in the taverns and hostelries. Galician nurses
probably regaled him with folk tales and ghost stories, and certainly he heard many pious *exempla* in the sermons of bishops

and preachers and even from the mouths of mendicant friars in village squares and at crossroads.[4]

Many libraries contained the more modern books, those written in the vernacular tongues—French, Provençal, Italian, German, Spanish, and Catalan—for these languages had by then developed literatures of their own. Some of these books were no more than translations from the Latin classics or from the sacred writings of the Church and the Bible, but others can be regarded as creative works, the writings of authors of originality. Spain's national literature, not very far advanced in the previous century, was in the thirteenth century past mere beginnings and well along the way to the literary flowering of Alfonso's reign. What has survived from those times may have had a strong influence upon the king's own work, whether on his original writings or on those he caused to be translated. It will be well, therefore, to examine the Spanish literary panorama prior to his reign and, when possible, to indicate influence upon Alfonsine productions.[5]

I *Lyric Poetry*

Modern scholarship reveals that most of the familiar genres of literature existed in Spain from early times. Lyric poetry, however, until fairly recently, could not be discovered prior to the late twelfth and early thirteenth centuries in Spanish. Of late, scholars have found that Spanish lyrics existed as the *jarchas* of the Andalusian Mozarabs as early as the middle of the ninth century. The *jarchas* are preserved only as additions at the end of Arabic *muashahas,* a variety of erudite Arabic poetry much used by the Andalusian Arabs and Moors. The point is that the *jarchas* were Spanish folk poems and existed orally. That they were gathered by the Moors and added as bits of local color to Arabic poems is not what is important: what matters is that they existed at all, for that they did proves that Spaniards composed lyric verse from early times. The Mozarabs, fleeing from the persecution of the Almorávides, and later of the Almohades, would certainly have carried their folk songs along with them to the North. Such lyrics as the *jarchas,* then, would have been transplanted to Castile, León, and Aragon by the Mozarabs.[6]

Just why any one should doubt that Castilians and Leonese themselves could have created lyric verse is difficult to understand, for folk poetry can develop anywhere and, more pertinently, there is strong reason to believe that the early lyrics of Galicia sprang up in that area independently, later to be mingled with the poetry of Provence in days of the troubadours. And yet some scholars refuse to credit the existence of early Castilian lyric poetry and say that Castile, hard pressed by the Moor, found time only for bellicose epics and the poetry of chivalric deeds. Has any people failed to develop love lyrics and folk songs? This author knows of none. Be that as it may, Prince Alfonso in his youth and early manhood knew lyric poetry and followed the lyric traditions of Galician-Portuguese troubadours. Such influence upon him was almost unavoidable, for this was the poetry most in vogue in his own century and for at least two centuries to come. Some two thousand poems, written by some two hundred different poets, survive from that period in three vast *cancioneros* or books of songs.[7] Every one who had any pretensions at all to poetry emulated the troubadours of Galicia and composed verses in Galician. Few Spaniards ever wrote in Castilian in the Middle Ages, at least when they composed lyrics.

A few, however, chose Spanish and Aragonese, and one of these created some of the loveliest of all medieval lyrics. The poet's name is not known, but the poem, called *Razón de Amor,* "Lay of Love," remains immortal.[8] In it we find a graphic example of a thirteenth-century manifestation of the troubadour school of courtly verse. Doubtless many such courtly lyrics existed in Alfonso's day, and he must certainly have read many, possibly even the *Razón de Amor.* In addition, poetic contests were held in France and Spain, and the court of King Ferdinand and later of Alfonso X, provided the backdrop for such exhibitions of poetic skill.

II *Narrative Poetry:* Mester de Juglaría

Since most lyric poetry written in Spain, even by Spaniards, was couched in the language of Galicia, a dialect of Portuguese, and since what Castilian poetry existed was principally narrative rather than lyric, scholars have been inclined to give primary importance to narrative verse. Indeed, the first piece of Spanish literature of importance, the *Poema de Mío Cid,*[9] "Lay of My Cid," is purely narrative, that is, it was almost surely meant to be delivered orally, chanted by bards, and there is strong likelihood that it could have been heard in the thirteenth century. This poem, considered by some to be a medieval epic, by others as a rhymed chronicle and, of late, by still others as perhaps a separate genre entirely—possibly a novelesque romance in verse—is the sole survivor of Spain's so-called epic. It is a magnificent work, imaginative, realistic, filled with empathy and characterization, and may rightly be called one of the great classics of Spanish literature. It is written in the style of irregular syllabication of the *mester de juglaría,* "the minstrel's school of versification," although an effort was made to produce lines of sixteen syllables, divided into two *laisses* of eight syllables each. Assonance, or vowel-rhyme was employed, not full-rhyme. Such poetry was becoming archaic in Alfonso's time, just as the epics themselves were losing in popularity, but even so the king could, on occasion, have heard one of these venerable pieces recited.

In addition to the *Poema de Mío Cid,* there exists a fragment of another long narrative poem in the *mester de juglaría.* This, called *Roncesvalles,* is all that is left today of what was a poetic treatment of Charlemagne's invasion of Spain and of the disaster that befell his peers, Roland and Oliver, as they formed the rear guard of the French army leaving Spain through the Pass of Roncesvalles. From the one hundred lines or so that have survived in a sole manuscript one gathers that it must have been a worthy member of the family of epico-narrative poems so popular in twelfth-century Spain. No other examples of the epic-like poems exist, but there were at one time cycles of these poems.[10] One can read them only in prosification as they appear in the thirteenth-century chronicles and in the *Primera Crónica General* produced under Alfonso's own patronage. His familiarity with his country's epic arts, then, was close.

Alfonso probably knew the *mester de juglaría* from another kind of poetry, the saint's life and the stories of other pious people. As early as the late twelfth century or the beginning years of the thirteenth, clerics had been using the *mester,* or at least a kind of poetry closely resembling it, for such works as *La Vida de Santa María Egipcíaca* and *El Libro dels Tres Reis d'Orient.*[11] The former was probably drawn from the Old French *Vie de Sainte Marie l'Egyptienne,* rather than from one of the Latin versions available, illustrating the fact that already one vernacular could serve as the basis of translation into another. When such translations made their way into Spanish, indeed even when the translation was made from Arabic, Latin, or Greek, original touches of the author-translator were often added. When Alfonso made translations, or had them done at his behest, we shall see that such originality was usually in evidence. The *Libro dels Tres Reis d'Orient* begins with the coming of the Magi Kings to visit the Christ child but soon moves on to the adventures of the Holy Family on its flight into Egypt. In both of these religious pieces, in fact in the *Poema de Mío Cid* and in medieval literature in general, the element of realism played an important role, and when Alfonso directed literary production, realism continued to appear. The use of folksy dialogue, of humor and direct discourse from the writer to his public, all contributed to vernacular writing, and may well have served the Learned King and his collaborators as models for their own compositions.

III *The New Narrative Poetry:* Mester de Clerecía

Sometime in the first quarter of the thirteenth century the style of long narrative poetry changed, replacing the *mester de juglaría*. This new versification was known as the *mester de clerecía*, "the cleric's school of versification," and those who wrote it prided themselves upon its regularity of syllabication—always lines of fourteen syllables—and its use of monorhymed quatrains rather than assonance. It was to become a very widely used form, and secular poets as well as clerics made use of it. An epic-type poem entitled *Poema de Fernán González*,[12] which related the adventures of the founder of Castile's independence from León, appeared in the new poetry. Alfonso certainly must have known of this piece and probably had read it, for its content in prosification is contained in the *Primera Crónica General*. He knew also the long and encyclopedic *Libro de Alexandre*,[13] which relates the life of Alexander the Great and assembles between its covers a prodigious volume of medieval lore and belief. In the same tradition was another poem in the *mester de clerecía*, also familiar to the Learned King. This was the account of the life of Apollonius of Tyre and his remarkably clever daughter, Tarsiana. It bears the title, *Libro de Apolonio*,[14] and it may be regarded as the first of the so-called Greek or Byzantine romances to appear in Spanish.

But the most famous and the most typically Spanish of all the poets who employed the new narrative verse was a parish priest named Gonzalo de Berceo, who flourished probably from the late twelfth century to about 1246. This poet, the first whose name we know in the history of Spanish literature, seems to have spent a quiet and peaceful life far from the activity of the cities and the court. In remote Berceo, tucked away in the Diocese of Calahorra in Old Castile, he produced a truly copious volume of writing. His interest and vocation was the veneration of the Blessed Virgin whose praises he sang and whose miracles he recounted in a collection of twenty-five poems; but the lives of Spanish saints native to his region also interested him, and he translated three of these from their lives written in Latin some centuries before his time. One was the *Vida de Santo Domingo de Silos*, "Life of St. Dominic of Silos," a miracle-worker of renown, who at last became the abbot of Berceo's beloved monastery, which bears the saint's name. A second relates the life of another saintly man who governed the other religious house dear to the poet. This was the *Vida de San Millán de la Cogolla*, "Life of St. Aemelianus of Cogolla"; the last is the *Vida de Santa Oria*, "Life of St. Aurea," a truly inspired poem, which not only tells of the saint's miracles while on earth but describes her reception when she arrived in heaven. These long pieces by Berceo could well have influenced the writings of the Learned King, as could and almost certainly did Berceo's *Milagros de Nuestra Señora*, mentioned previously.[15]

Berceo read Latin well and was a good translator, but this does not mean that he lacked originality. When one considers that he was able to render the wooden and antique style of the Latin versions of the three saints' lives into a Castilian of considerable beauty and primitive charm, one comes to esteem his originality. His use of dialogue, homespun humor, empathy, and local color, made rich by employing the kind of language found among farmers and woodsmen, added much to Castilian writing and could have set Alfonso a model for the style of some of his

Cantigas de Santa María. And Berceo's active effort to obtain rapport with his public certainly is echoed in some of the miracles later recited by Alfonso.

It is interesting to speculate upon the possibility of actual personal contact between the rustic poet of San Millán de la Cogolla and Santo Domingo de Silos and the sophisticated and learned Alfonso. Both composed collections of Our Lady's miracles; both lived in an age of faith and believed in the ability and willingness of the Virgin to intervene in man's affairs; and each in his own way tried to teach that faith in her would save mankind. From the *Cantigas* we know that the king actually visited numerous shrines where miracles took place so as to verify them and study their background. Would he not have visited Berceo, a man who had written probably the first collection of such miracles in the Spanish language? The haunts of Berceo were not strange to Alfonso.

We have written evidence that he visited the monastery of Santo Domingo de Silos in 1255 not more than ten years after Berceo's death.[16] This visit was made even in the midst of the revolt against the king when his brother, Enrique, tried to take his kingdom. Alfonso remained there for eight days, praying and asking the intervention of Santo Domingo in the outcome of the war. Indeed, the monk who witnessed the subsequent events wrote of the saint's answer made to Alfonso in a dream or vision and of the wealth bestowed by the grateful monarch when his prayer was answered. Might not Alfonso have betaken himself to Berceo to visit the aging poet of the *Milagros* so as to learn firsthand his techniques and possible additional miraculous lore? Alfonso, recall, was born in 1221. Berceo lived at least as late as 1246, after which date his name ceases to appear in monastic rosters. There was ample opportunity and time to permit the crossing of their paths.

IV *The Debates*

Berceo's contribution to pious writing—the lives of saints and the miracles of the Virgin—when added to the earlier accounts of saints and holy personages represented by the life of St. Mary the Egyptian and the flight of the Holy Family into Egypt, all but complete the roster of pious writing. However, there were two other genres popular in the thirteenth century and both would have been familiar to Alfonso. One of these was the debate, common in other vernacular literatures outside of Spain and, of course, in Latin in which language debates were first written. In them two characters argue, usually in favor of their own merits. Water debates with wine about which is the more valuable in the sacraments in the poem known as the *Denuestos del Agua e el Vino*, "Reproaches of Water and Wine," of the early thirteenth century; another, entitled *Disputa del Alma e el Cuerpo*, "Dispute of the Soul and the Body," is a lively discussion about physical and worldly excellence as opposed to spiritual and heavenly; a third is known as *Elena e María* and deals with the relative merits of a knight and a cleric in the eyes of their sweethearts. The type was apparently very popular, for it had dramatic possibilities, and the various debates and disputes may have been intended for oral handling with two people acting out the parts. Such poems lived beyond the end of the century.[17]

V *Drama*

The last genre associated with religion was drama. Alfonso must have seen many plays, for they were presented in all the churches at certain seasons of the Christian calendar, especially at Easter and Christmas. The well-known development of church drama, age-old, and by Alfonso's time often quite intricate was, of course, represented in the Iberian Peninsula both in Latin and the vernacular form. However, only two plays have survived the ages, and of these but one is available in a usable edition. This is the so-called *Auto de los Reyes Magos*,[18] "Drama of the Magi Kings," of the late twelfth or early thirteenth century. It belongs, of course, to the Nativity Cycle of medieval drama. In it one finds again the element of Castilian realism, of life and movement and even touches of wry humor. The other surviving example is a play based upon the Assumption of the Virgin. To this day such a play is presented in Elche at the Feast of the Assumption; it probably had its beginnings in the Middle Ages.

Alfonso knew about secular drama also and apparently eschewed it. In the first division of his code of laws, *Las Siete Partidas*, he devoted considerable space to both legitimate drama, that is, pious drama, and to illegal or reprehensible plays, which are referred to as *juegos de escarnio,* "farcical pieces." Mere mention of such plays is enough to prove their existence, which is important to an understanding of the state of medieval Spanish literature.

VI *Proverbs*

The last two varieties of Spanish writing often appear linked together, although they were often independent of one another. Proverbs in collections, and as minor parts of prose narratives, were extremely well esteemed in medieval Spain. Various collections of proverbs and proverbial wisdom are extant, and more must certainly have existed. Among the most important are *Flores de Filosofía,* "Flowers of Philosophy," which claimed to contain all the wisdom of thirty-seven ancient philosophers, including Seneca; another was *Poridad de Poridades,* "Secret of Secrets," also known as *Castigos de Aristótil a Alexandre,* "Instructions of Aristotle for Alexander," which was a Spanish version of the *Secreta Secretorum,* "Secret of Secrets." Still a third was the *Bonium* or *Bocados de Oro,* "Morsels of Gold," from an Arabic original, which contains two letters apocryphally attributed to Alexander the Great. The *Libro de los Cien Capitulos,* "Book of the One Hundred Chapters," belonged to the same sources.[19]

VII *Brief Narrative in Prose*

The other variety of writing, more oriental than even the proverb, which Alfonso knew and loved, was the brief narrative—fable, apologue, folk tale and *fabliau.* So attracted was he to this genre that the first of his literary works was a translation of a noted eastern book, long known in the East, the Arabic *Kalila wa-Dimna,* written in Baghdad about 750 by a Moslem erudite named Abdallah ben Al-muqaffa. This writer was not so much an author as a translator and transmitter, for large parts of *Kalila wa-Dimna* can be traced back through Persian books to the Hindu *Panchatantra,* one of the great monuments of late Sanskrit letters. This important oriental work, a strange mingling of wisdom, philosophy, proverb, and fiction, Alfonso assigned to translators. He received the result of their labors in 1251, the year before that of his coronation.[20] He was a prince, then, both when the Spanish version was undertaken and when it was completed. A detailed discussion of the Castilian translation appears in the next chapter.

In the second year of his reign his brother, Fadrique, caused another collection of oriental tales to be rendered into Castilian. This was called in Spanish *El Libro de los Engaños e Asaya-mientos de las Mugeres*, "The Book of the Wiles and Tricks of Women." Since it belonged to the famous family of books descending from the oriental *Book of Sindibad* (refering to some-one other than the Sinbad the Sailor of the *Arabian Nights*), it was another landmark in western writing.[21]

A third book from the East, employed in revised form by the Church long before Alfonso's time to teach moral lessons, was *Barlaam and Josephat*,[22] found in Greek and Latin and in all the western vernaculars, including Spanish. It is actually a Christian-ization of the life of Buddha. Its impact upon the West was truly phenomenal, for its tales were utilized by many authors, among them Alfonso's nephew, Prince Don Juan Manuel, and later Cal-derón and Shakespeare.

CHAPTER 4

Alfonso X and Eastern Fiction:
Calila e Digna

I *Brief Narrative Before* Calila e Digna

WHEN Prince Alfonso in the year 1251 received from the hands of his translators the Spanish version of the Arabic *Kalila wa-Dimna,* he was repeating an historic literary tradition of great antiquity. Kings all across the East from as far away as India had caused this book, or versions and sections of it, to be transcribed in their own languages. Nor was the process to end with the Learned King. But before considering Alfonso's famous *Calila e Digna,* the first translation of oriental fiction into a western vernacular tongue, it would be well to view what brief fiction Europe had produced and which might have come to his attention. If the study of Alfonso's contribution to Spanish and European fiction is important, also important is the fictional potential of the West before he enriched it. Accordingly, the first part of this chapter will examine the development of western fiction, in both prose and verse, prior to Alfonso's contribution. When we turn to *Calila e Digna,* and oriental brief fiction, more emphasis will be placed on prose narrative since prose was the preferred vehicle of the East.

Apparently tales in European literature appeared first in verse. We have already seen that the earliest tales in Spanish—saints' lives, miracles of the Virgin, and accounts of other pious individuals—were versified. In this, Spain was but following a western tradition which seemed to have regarded poetry as the only literary medium of value. Even such scurrilous material as that making up the *fabliaux* were written in thirteenth-century Picard verse.

Spaniards have from their beginnings loved short stories and fables. Their literature abounds in *cuentos* or brief narratives of all kinds, and in this genre some of the finest authors of the Spanish-speaking world have made their greatest contributions. Even the *Poema de Mío Cid,* regarded by many as a great epic poem, contains a few germs of brief narrative. And after the poem was set down in writing—in 1140—the popularity of the short story continued to increase. Alfonso X would have no small part to play in the development and perfecting of tales, aided to some extent by his family; the King, as well as his relatives, would borrow much from eastern tales and would have many of these translated into their native language.

The history of fiction reveals clearly that every culture, no matter how primitive or civilized, has created and cultivated brief narratives of various sorts, particularly the fable. Aesop and the tradition for which he is famous influenced Greece from pre-classical times throughout the entire Hellenic Period. Phaedrus and other Roman cultivators of the fable perpetuated Aesopic conventions within the Roman world during its long domination. Graeco-Roman fables flowed uninterrupted into the Middle Ages to become one of the favorite readings of medieval man, as evidenced in the *Ysopets,* books of Aesopic-type fables popular everywhere, both in Latin and in the vernaculars. Nor would the love of fable end here. The revival of learning instituted a vigorous flowering of brief fiction in the Renaissance and kept it alive for later ages. Greece had not been the only ancient nation to cultivate this genre. All the great civilizations of antiquity—Egypt, Babylon, Assyria, to name a few—had known and loved fables; and these stories live on today in the folktales of their descendants, long after their cities have crumbled into ruins and rubble. The same is true farther east, in India especially, whose treasury of story is the richest in the world. And anthropologists have proved that the bushmen of Australia and the most uncivilized of African tribes have nurtured, and continue to cherish, fables, making them an integral part of their culture and wisdom.

With the fall of the Western Roman Empire, some fables of the classical world survived the holocaust and were bequeathed to the citizens of the early Middle Ages. To these the Church, which from its beginnings had sponsored parables, added its *exempla* or moralizing tales, in those early times written in Latin.

Stories from many sources eventually were included, thereby en-riching the European store; but the richest sources were the great collections of tales recounting the lives and adventures of the saints and the holy hermits who dwelt in the deserts of Upper Egypt and in Asia Minor. The *Vitae Patrum*, "Lives of the Church Fathers," is one of the largest and most representative of such monkish collections. However, the Church was also the preserver of the classical heritage, and therefore gathered and refurbished the fables of the Ancient World, attaching new and Christian moralizations to these pagan tales. Such collections were in the Spanish libraries, and Alfonso certainly was brought up on many of them.

In the period immediately following the collapse of Rome, and with increasing vigor in the Middle Ages, more native tales were gathered and worked by medieval man into interesting cycles. In England there was the Arthurian Cycle, soon to permeate all Europe and well-known in Alfonsine Spain. In France appeared the *Lays* of Marie de France, a group of tales inspired in Celtic folklore and tradition. In France, too, probably were born the beast epic and the Cycle of Renart the Fox, whose traditions sprang from classical and native sources; fragments of these were known in Spain. By the thirteenth century the *fabliau* had arisen in Picardy, tracing its origins back into the folklore of the region, but spiced also with motifs from other heritages, including some eastern ones. And tales from Germanic and Scandinavian sagas had drifted down into the main current of European fiction. Western Europe's corpus of fiction was rich, indeed, and yet by the thirteenth century it was ready for a new transfusion.

This new vitalization was supplied to Europe by the East. Contacts with the eastern story were fairly numerous, but the most important channels of transmission from the Orient to the Occident were these: Moorish culture in Spain, which maintained constant contacts with the seats of Moslem learning; the thou-sands of returning crusaders and their retainers, as well as mer-chants who traded in the East; and lastly, the Christian clergy who were beginning to incorporate oriental fables with greater frequency into their collections of *exempla*. These three channels, together with lesser streams and rivulets of eastern tales, went far toward revolutionizing the course of the western short narra-

Alfonso X and Eastern Fiction: Calila e Digna

tive. Without these oriental contributions Boccaccio, Don Juan Manuel, Marguerite of Navarre, Chaucer, Rabelais, and scores of other writers would never have been able to recount some of their best tales.

The Moslems, then, whether in Spain, Egypt or the Middle East, were the true transmitters of the eastern story. They were collectors, too, and their most polished assemblage was the *Thousand Nights and a Night*, structured upon Persian and Hindu repositories of tales. All that was exciting, lewd, romantic, or in any way interesting went into this remarkable panorama of literary and folkloristic narratives. Erudites of the Moslem world viewed such collections publicly with disdain, but in privacy devoured them with zeal. Among such books was the work of Abdallah ben Almuqaffa whose *Kalila wa-Dimna* later served Alfonso X so well.

II Kalila wa-Dimna *and* Calila e Digna

Both the extant manuscripts of *El Libro de Calila e Digna,* "Book of Calila and Digna," state in their colophons that the book was a translation made at the behest of King Alfonso, and a third manuscript, now lost, is reported by reliable authorities to have claimed the same royal patronage.[1] Just why some scholars have preferred not to accept Alfonso's patronage as a perfectly legitimate declaration is not easy to determine. A. G. Solalinde, who made an edition of the book based upon both existing manuscripts, believed that some copyist attributed *Calila e Digna* to the Learned King because he hoped that such attribution would lend the translation an aura of dignity and authority. Now many cases of apocryphal attribution have been recorded, but I fail to see why Alfonso's book should be included among them.

A tradition in the royal family seems to confirm Alfonso's patronage—that of sponsoring the translation of bodies of oriental fable and story. We have already seen that this happened in the case of Prince Fadrique who caused the *Libro de los Engaños* to be taken from Arabic. This patronage is clearly stated in the book's prefatory remarks, to wit: "The Prince considered it meet and was pleased to have this book translated out of Arabic into Castilian to forewarn those deceived by the wiles of women. This book was translated in 1253."[2] Scholars accept Prince Fadrique's patronage of an eastern collection of tales, and surely no one has suggested that its attribution to him, irresponsible and unstudious as he was, was made in any attempt to give this book an atmosphere of dignity or authority. Then there is the case of Alfonso's son, that same rebellious Sancho, who ruled as Sancho IV after the Learned King's death, and who caused another collection of tales to be set down. The title of this fourteenth-century book is *Castigos e Documentos para Bien Vivir*, "Teachings and Documents for the Good Life," and in it, along with tales of western provenance, are oriental stories and fables.[3] No one has argued that authority would accrue to a book through its attribution to that violent and unartistic man. One further example of a work created by a member of Alfonso's family should suffice. Alfonso's nephew, Don Juan Manuel, wrote what is now considered to be the classic of medieval Spanish tales, *El Conde Lucanor*, "Count Lucanor," or *Libro de Patronio*, "Book of Patronio," which is a collection of some fifty stories, most of which are of eastern origin.[4] If, then, Alfonso's brother, his son and his nephew either patronized or sponsored such books or, as in the case of Don Juan Manuel, composed them, it seems only logical to accept the King himself as the sponsor of *Calila e Digna*. Everything fits: the affection of Alfonso for oriental culture; the need to place the "best sellers" of the times—Arabic tales—within the reach of Spaniards who could not read them in the original; and lastly, the feeling that it was a thing demanded by ancient precept and tradition. Alfonso knew that an Indian monarch had caused most of the stories to be assembled and set down in the language of India, that a Persian king had the Hindu original rendered into Persian, and that a Moslem king in Araby had caused its translation into that language. All this is plainly stated in the Introduction of Abdallah ben Almuqaffa. The Learned King was performing a duty, as it were, in perpetuating the heritage of the past.

III   *The Function of* Calila e Digna

Alfonso X had a further reason for translating the Arabic *Kalila wa-Dimna*.[5] This was the didactic function of the book, or possibly the pseudodidactic. A very ancient convention, going as far back as Aesop, insisted that stories should teach as well as entertain. If in the previous discussion I have seemed to place

[52]

too much stress upon the recreational value of eastern stories, I have done so in the interest of literary history. I have not intended to deny the didactic side of the matter, for the instructional element was certainly present. In medieval Europe and Asia, story and moralization went hand in hand. As to which—story or moralization—first motivated stories no one knows. It can be argued, probably to no successful conclusion, that people who enjoyed entertaining tales gathered them as purely recreational reading, and that later moralizations were attached; on the other hand there is support for the idea that the utilitarian end was the important thing, and that moralists selected stories for the purpose of illustrating given lessons. As in most arguments, there are always two sides, and stories were assembled for reasons both instructional as well as recreational. And, of course, in the Middle Ages some books without any doubt served both functions. Alfonso's nephew, Don Juan Manuel, best sums up the case for this compromise. In the introduction to his *Conde Lucanor* he says that doctors always mix something sweet with the bitter medicine needed by the liver, so that the liver will accept it; and that he wrote his book in the same manner, so that those who read it could enjoy it, if they liked, or might obtain moral advice and precept intermixed with the sweetness of the stories in it.

By these observations the King's nephew might have had the last word on the subject, except for the fact that not all such books are enlightening, uplifting, or moral in their content. Some are no more than repositories of gay and often obscene fictions to which no valuable moral can possibly be attached. Take, for example, *The Book of the Wiles of Women,* translated at the behest of Prince Fadrique, Alfonso's brother. Its preface clearly states that the Prince had it translated out of Arabic to forewarn those deceived by the wiles of women. It purports to be a series of didactic tales, each with a moralization, but surely no one could take seriously the kind of lessons it presents. Everything in the actual content of this book indicates that it was put together for entertainment, with a didactic reason given tongue-in-cheek for added levity. Surely no one who reads these stories today can believe that they were intended to be serious. Spaniards—as well as Arabs, and Persians and Hindus before them—must have reacted in much the same way we do today. Humor lay even in the very claim to didacticism; the humor was intentional and was, perhaps, the very genius of this peculiar inversion of the time-honored ends of art.

This leads to a factor that westerners often overlook, when they examine oriental fiction, although if they stopped to consider it, the same element exists at times in western fiction. Moralizations in the East were deliberately attached to some stories to give an excuse for their presence in books. In other words, erudite people, even kings, priests, and philosophers, can read books of wisdom without criticism, whereas the reading of light fiction, such as the tales found in *Calila e Digna,* might cause brows to raise. But if these scholarly minds read books that affected to be the wisdom of the ages, that offered profound views of life, and purported to be serious and learned writings, no blame could accrue. If these intellectual tomes contained—for the purpose of illustration, of course—certain farcical, naughty, light, and otherwise purely entertaining tales, who could blame the serious reader? In the beginning the argument may have actually been as simple as this. But as time went on and as people became more sophisticated, it no longer rang true, and so the humorous and witty sophism of accepting it as truth was born.

In time, then, a subtle casuistry became one of the underlying principles of fabulistic writing. Such casuistry had existed in Arabic culture as early as the translation of *Kalila wa-Dimna* from the Persian. Indeed the translator is regarded as the prime mover of its acceptance into the Moslem world. For Abdallah ben Almuqaffa, a Persian by birth and a Zoroastrian until his conversion to Islam, was a very logical transmitter of both the casuistry and the actual stories. Learned Moslems took delight, then, in a sophisticated philosophy of belles-lettres known as *adab,* a word all but impossible to translate into English or any other western language.[6] This system made it possible for the most scholarly and even the most pious people to discuss a wide range of subjects and read a wide range of literary genres. Under the disguise of mock-seriousness, they could chuckle at life and its foibles, while they pretended to ponder a purportedly weighty content. Much of this *adab* must have passed over in translation and, indeed, through actual personal association with the Moslem savants of Spain, into Alfonso's court. The idea that it did not reach the king and his intellectuals can hardly be accepted, for that group kept a harmonious rapport with oriental culture and learning and could hardly have been so naïve as to overlook or misunderstand anything so delightfully sophisticated as *adab.*

Most probably Alfonso and his translators saw through the speciousness of the openly declared *raison d'être* of *Calila e Digna* and *El Libro de los Engaños* and hoped that the Spaniards who would read these books would also savor their ambiguous complexion.

And yet, it is also possible that they took a serious view of the volumes and their moralizations which, after all, at least in the case of *Calila e Digna,* if not of Prince Fadrique's book, could be regarded as earnest and straightforward. The entire question is tantalizing, for its solution would shed much light upon the very thinking of medieval Spaniards. It is likely that Alfonso and the sophisticates at his court realized that any book could have a variety of meanings. They would have agreed, one suspects, with Cervantes who, some three centuries later, in speaking of his own masterpiece, would have Samson Carrasco say about it: ". . . children turn its pages, youths read it, grown men understand it and old folk delight in it; and finally, it is so read and known by a variety of people that scarcely do they see some rawboned nag than they say, 'there goes Rocinante.'" [7]

And look at the fate of *Alice in Wonderland,* which Lewis Carroll hardly meant to become a children's classic. *Calila e Digna* in Alfonsine Spain might have had two, or perhaps even several aims, if directed toward a varied audience of readers. The range might have run all the way from philosophers, who probably read it for fun, to men and women, yes, and children, too, who simply wanted the pleasure to be derived from delightful fables and piquant tales. Today the Spanish version of Abdallah ben Almuqaffa's masterpiece is read primarily by students of literature and language, but many of its tales are to be found on the shelves of children alongside juvenile versions of *Aesop's Fables, King Arthur,* or the *Arabian Nights' Entertainment.* Editions of the fables of *Kalila wa-Dimna,* I am told by a Moslem friend from Cairo, formed a part of his childhood books, much as the stories of *Uncle Remus* formed a part of mine.

Alfonso X, then, when he made *Calila e Digna* available to the

western reader, opened the door to eastern fable. The influence
of the volume upon later writers in Spain is simply incalculable,
from the point of view of content as well as from that of a fresh
oriental style and presentation of brief narrative. Such may have
been the functions and purposes of *Calila e Digna,* which perpetuated in thirteenth-century Spain the book's tradition in the
Hindu, Persian, and Arabic cultures.

IV *The Form and the Content*

The structure of *Calila e Digna* is like that of so many oriental
books written in the Middle Ages and earlier. *The Panchatantra,*[8]
from which most of the Persian, the Arabic, and the Spanish
versions came, was divided into five long *tantras* or divisions.
Each of these parts was in actuality a kind of novel or was at least
novelesque. Each was of considerable length, had a set of major
and minor characters, a plot, and a logical denouement. In other
words, most of the chapters in *The Panchatantra* were frame
stories into which the writer interpolated numerous fables or
short stories, each with its own characters and plot. Some confusion is occasioned for western readers by the fact that the characters in the frame story relate the interpolated tales, and that
within those tales still other characters speak and tell still other
stories. Tales within tales within tales are difficult to unravel,
but the eastern reader seemed to accept this arrangement and
so, apparently, did the medieval Spaniard, for *Calila e Digna*
certainly follows the ancient structure and form of *The Panchatantra.*

Most of *The Panchatantra* appears in both *Calila e Digna*[9] and
Kalila wa-Dimna, and without doubt was in the Persian rendition.
The Arabic version of ben Almuqaffa, however, added a brief
preface by Ali, the son of Alschah Faresi (not found in the Spanish translation) and a rather long account of the journey of the
Persian, Burzoe, who was sent by his king to India and who
returned with a Persian translation of *The Panchatantra.* Doubtless the Arabic translator had this part before him when he began. He also added an Introduction of his own, which is one of
his original contributions. It is a long philosophical tract which
begins with a statement that all good learning and wisdom are
the heritage of the wise men of the past. This Introduction goes

on to explain that it is a man's duty to study and learn, but also to work and gain; that he is not to trust other men, lest they deceive him; and most important of all is that practical wisdom which serves man in this life on earth and in the preparation for the life after death. Into this tract ben Almuqaffa inserted no less than nine short *exempla*, each of which is illustrative of what happens when a man is gullible, thoughtless, hasty in action, or simple-minded or ignorant. Here, I believe, one can discern strong indications of that mock-seriousness mentioned earlier. In the Spanish translation of this tract, by the way, there is little deviation from the Arabic. The translators did, however, omit three of the interpolated stories; whether owing to their own criteria or because they were using a copy of ben Almuqaffa lacking these tales, is unknown.

Immediately after ben Almuqaffa's Introduction there is a section in *Calila e Digna* entitled COMMO EL REY DESERBE (in the other manuscript it is EL REY SIRECHUEL) ENVIO A BERZEBUEY A TIERRA DE INDIA, "How King Dixerbe (or Syrechuel) Sent Berzebuey to the Land of India." This, I regard as Chapter I of the Spanish *Calila e Digna*. In it one reads of the famous Persian physician sent by his king to India to find herbs reputed to revive the dead. After a year the herbs are found, but none of the dead are resuscitated, and Berzebuey is in disgrace; however, Hindu doctors explain that the herbs are actually books of wisdom, the medicines are good teachings of the philosophers, and the dead to be revived are the ignorant, who can only be brought to life by education. Berzebuey then returns with the books which he has translated into Persian from Hindi and is honored by his king and his people. The section ends with this statement: "And one of those writings was that book which they call *Calila e Digna.*"

The next section is entitled LA HISTORIA DEL MEDICO BERZEBUEY, "The Story of Doctor Berzebuey," which constitutes Chapter II in the Spanish text. It is the autobiography of the Persian physician and therefore told in the first person. It was in all probability translated by ben Almuqaffa and, hence, saved from oblivion by him. It relates interesting and valuable material, for in it one reads of the education of a young eastern nobleman, of his years with his tutors, and of how he surpassed

all his fellow students. Armed with the best of educations, Berzebuey undertook the study of medicine and at last became a practicing physician of renown. But doubts about the reason for man's
life on earth assailed him and led him to conclude that the best of
doctors was the one who worked, not for gain and praise, but for
the sake of the soul in preparation for its entry into heaven. Even
here he was uncertain, and he set out accordingly to read the
works of the authorities in every field of endeavor, only to learn
that they all were self-interested, even those who practiced religion. To illustrate how easy it is for a man to be deceived by his
fellows, Berzebuey inserted five tales, whose moralizations are
more calculated to instill despair in the human soul than to com-
fort it. Here again the mock-seriousness of *adab* seems to penetrate the veil of didacticism.

Berzebuey ends his autobiography by saying that he at last
resolved his problems by preparing for the world to come, and
that he hoped the lessons he brought back in his book—he can
mean only his translation of *The Panchatantra*—would serve his
fellow man.

This remarkable piece of autobiography—sophisticated, quite
possibly imbued with a wry skepticism, and subject to the accu-
sation of *double-entendre*—seems at first glance to be out of place
in the works of Alfonso, a king who believed deeply in everything that Christianity taught. Not one of Berzebuey's moralizations is pious or unselfish, since they all teach self-interest, practical wisdom of the kind designed to save one from the deceits
of others or how to gain advantage over one's adversaries by
tricks and ruses positively unethical for the most part. Such wisdom belongs more to the East than to the Christian West, and
would seem to go all the way back to the Hindu *Panchatantra*
for its roots. Open admission, bald and unashamed, is offered in
the Introduction to the Indian classic. Vishnusharman, the greatest of the Hindu sages, asked by his king to instruct the monarch's
stupid sons, replies: "O King, listen. Here is the plain truth. I
am not the man to sell good learning for a hundred land-grants.
But if I do not, in six month's time, make the boys acquainted
with *the art of intelligent* living [italics mine], I will give up my
own good name." *The Panchatantra* was, then, admittedly a book
of practical guidance to the successful earthly life, although the

element of tongue-in-cheek moralization, even in India, was never absent. It belongs to the class of books known as *niti-shastra* writings, that is, books on the wise, but not necessarily the virtuous, conduct of life. The three most important ways to attain *niti*, "wise conduct," were: (1) the exercise of resolute action; (2) the gaining and keeping of friends; and (3) the proper use of intelligence. The aim and goal of *niti* was the attainment of the utmost joy from life *in the world of men* not, let it be noted, in the afterlife.

Such a philosophy could have arisen quite easily in India, where religion taught that Nirvana was the ultimate reward and that the survival of the personal and individual was not of importance. That the precepts of *niti*, whether understood or misunderstood, should have passed unchallenged into Persia, which held to the tenets of Zoroaster, and into Islam, which followed those of Mohammed, both predicated on a personal heaven, would be surprising but for two concepts. So powerful were these ideas, indeed, that they permitted a Christian prince like Alfonso to accept such an outlook in *Calila e Digna.* One was the mock-seriousness mentioned above which permitted readers to wink at the specious philosophizing found in the book; the second is that double standard present in even the most ethically motivated faiths, that is, the practical, callous, businesslike attitude associated with physical and financial survival.

The remaining sections of *Calila e Digna* will now be treated. The first, called THE CHAPTER OF THE LION AND THE BULL, is actually the third chapter in the Spanish text. It is a paraphrase of the first section of *The Panchatantra,* entitled THE LOSS OF FRIENDS. All but two of the twenty stories come from the thirty-three tales found in this section of the Hindu work. The chapter is the novelesque account of two jackals named Calila and Digna (in Sanskrit, Kaladaka and Damanaka) who serve in the court of the lion. Digna, an ambitious social climber, deceives the lion into killing Senceba, the bull, the lion's faithful friend. The twenty brief narratives are related by various characters to show the results of good and evil actions. Some of these have become famous in world literature, especially in Spanish letters. The novelesque frame story is itself a kind of satire on the courts of kings and is readable and interesting. Furthermore,

the many jewels of verse found in the Hindi, though not translated as verse, have nonetheless not been lost, for excellent prosi-
fications of these remain in the Spanish text. No doubt the Persian
rendition contained these also, though we cannot know for sure
whether or not ben Almuqaffa found them still in verse when
he set out to make his translation.

The second frame story, known as LA PESQUISA DE DIGNA,
"The Trial of Digna," which is Chapter IV in the Spanish book,
is not found in the Hindu source at all, may or may not have
formed a part of the Persian, and was, of course, in the Arabic.
In it there is a complicated and lengthy trial, rich in satire, and
as interesting to the medieval mind as it is to the modern, because of fascination with what goes on in courtrooms. Witnesses
are called to testify; investigations are made by courtiers who
are almost self-styled detectives; and the treacherous Digna is
sentenced to death by starvation. His innocent friend, Calila, who
tries constantly to dissuade him from mischief, dies of grief and
shame. Only four brief narratives appear in this section; since
none of them is in *The Panchatantra,* they must have been interpolated either by Berzebuey or ben Almuqaffa.

The next section in both the Arabic and Spanish versions constitutes Chapter V in the latter. It is derived from Book II of the
Hindu original entitled THE WINNING OF FRIENDS. Its
frame story is a pleasant beast-fable of a dove, a tortoise, a stag,
and a crow, who band together in friendship to defeat the plans
of a hunter. Its title is DE LA PALOMA COLORADA E DEL
GAMO E DEL CUERVO, E ES CAPITULO DE LOS PUROS
AMIGOS, "Of the Bright-hued Dove, and of the Tortoise, and
of the Stag and of the Crow, and It is a Chapter about Pure
Friends." Only three brief narratives, all also found in the Hindu
text appear, and all moralize on the virtue of making friends.

Calila e Digna's Chapter VI is entitled DE LOS CUERVOS
E DE LOS BUOS, "Of the Crows and Owls," and is a delightful
satire of men and war and of racial hatreds. In addition, it presents a character who is a double agent, a crow purportedly
driven out and badly hurt by his own people, who goes to the
owls and promises to lead them to victory against the crows. The
Sanskrit original in this sequence contained seventeen tales, the
Arabic had eight and the Spanish has nine.

[60]

Next appears Chapter VII in *Calila e Digna,* bearing the title DEL GALAPAGO E DEL XIMIO, "Of the Sea Turtle and the Ape," which stems from Book IV of *The Panchatantra,* THE LOSS OF GAINS, in which a crocodile plays the role of the sea turtle. To this day the tale is enjoyed by children, but in olden times it may have served as a satire on false friends. In it the ape and the sea turtle become friends, which annoys the latter's wife. Pretending to be ill and to be cured only by the heart of an ape, she persuades her husband to try to lure his anthropoid friend to his death. But the ape, learning of the trick as he rides on the turtle's back toward that reptile's island home, says that he has left his heart back on shore. When the stupid turtle takes him back to get it, the ape leaps to safety. *The Panchatantra* interpolated no less than eleven stories into this sequence, whereas *Calila e Digna* and the Arabic version inserted only one.

The next section of *Calila e Digna,* Chapter VIII, is actually little more than one single story taken from *The Panchatantra's* Book V, ILL-CONSIDERED ACTION, which in the original contains a full dozen brief narratives. This story, one of the best-known of the collection, tells of a woman who leaves her son in the care of a pet mongoose. A serpent comes to bite the child and is killed by the faithful animal which, in turn, is killed by the mother, thinking that the blood on the creature's muzzle is that of her child. Here the result of hasty and ill-considered action is seen at its worst. Only one inserted tale appears in this section but it is a famous one, the ancestor of that account of the milkmaid who counted her chickens before they were hatched. In the Hindu, Arabic, and Spanish versions, however, the pro-tagonist is a man, not a maid. The title in *Calila e Digna* is DEL RELIGIOSO E EL GATO, "Of the Holy Man and the Cat," owing to the fact that in the Spanish version the mongoose, an animal unknown in the Iberian Peninsula, has been replaced by a cat.

Chapters IX and X of the Spanish are very short tales, hardly enough to be regarded logically as chapters. The ninth, DEL GATO E DEL MUR, "Of the Cat and the Mouse," narrates the account of a mouse and a cat who help one another to escape their powerful foes; the tenth, entitled DEL REY BERAMER E DEL AVE QUE DIZEN CATRA, "Of King Beramer and the

Bird Named Catra," is a strange tale. The bird's son and the king's are reared together, but one day the prince wrings the baby bird's neck in a fit of rage. Catra, to punish him, pecks out both his eyes, and the king tries to pretend forgiveness so as to catch and kill her. It is to no avail, for Catra sees the danger and flies away.

Chapter XI, DEL REY CEDERANO E DEL SU ALGUAZIL E DE SU MUGER ELBED, "Of King Cederano, his Adviser, Beled, and his Wife, Elbed," is a tale of a palace intrigue, of soothsayers who attempt to persuade a monarch to kill his family and his friends, using a falsely interpreted dream to bring it all about. They are foiled. This is a romance which reads like something from *The Arabian Nights' Entertainment*. Only two tales are set within its frame, and neither frame story nor tales come from *The Panchatantra*.

The last four chapters are brief. Chapter XII, DEL ARQUERO E DE LA LEONA, "Of the Bowman and the Lioness," runs to only a page or so and has little plot; Chapter XIII, DEL RELI-GIOSO E DE SU HUESPED, "Of the Holy Man and his Guest," is a few lines of frame story used as the vehicle of probably the shortest tale in the entire book; Chapter XIV, DEL LEON E DEL LOBO CERVAL RELIGIOSO, "Of the Lion and the Pious Jackal," a well-plotted tale of a jackal too pious to kill for its food. The lion, with some effort, persuades the jackal to become a courtier. The story then progresses in a fashion much like the frame story of Chapter III about the lion and the bull and the two jackals, Calila and Digna. For the pious jackal, much like Senceba, the bull, though not killed, is almost destroyed by envious courtiers; Chapter XV, DEL ORENZE E DEL TASUGO E DE LA CULEBRA E DEL RELIGIOSO, "Of the Goldsmith, the Badger, the Snake, and the Holy Man," is a tale of beasts who repay a man's kindness, while the goldsmith who owes him as much, almost causes his death; and Chapter XVI, the last chapter in the Spanish version, DEL FIJO DEL REY E DEL FIDALGO E DE SUS COMPAÑEROS, "Of the King's Son and of the Hidalgo and of Their Companions," shows that each man must use those gifts given him by nature or society. Of these last four chapters only XIV and XV belong to *The Panchatantra*.

I have devoted much space to a rather detailed criticism and description of *El Libro de Calila e Digna,* not only because of the book's importance to the history of brief fiction in the West, but for other reasons as well. It helps us to understand the place of Moorish thought and attitude toward life; it reveals the way in which eastern literary tastes and philosophies were able to penetrate Spain and the West; it helps to measure the closeness of the cultural contacts between the court of the Learned King and the East, through Moorish Spain; and it exemplifies the kind of oriental themes, motifs, and stories which could successfully cross linguistic, religious, racial, and geographical frontiers. It catches the young Alfonso at a time when his youthful interests in stories may have been at its peak, and it brings a literary touch to his scientifically-historically-juridically overtoned production. *Calila e Digna,* the *Cantigas de Santa María,* and the *Cantigas Profanas* form the corpus of his strictly literary outpouring.

CHAPTER 5

The Cantigas de Santa María

I *Alfonso's Affinity with the* Cantigas

SUPERLATIVES begin to come to mind when the *Cantigas de Santa María*, "Canticles of Holy Mary," are mentioned. And superlatives mount when one reflects that these *cantigas,* or canticles, to use an English equivalent, are the apogee of perfection in three distinct artistic media. In the area of pictorial art they are unsurpassed in the excellence of their marvellously colored miniatures and illuminations; unmatched in variety and beauty in their music; and unequaled in their literary and thematic content and manner of presentation. It is reasonable to believe that Alfonso expended more time and money upon the production of the *Cantigas de Santa María* than upon any of his other contributions. The *Cantigas* have been called the most clear, accurate, and faithful witness of thirteenth-century life and belief; the most noble attempt to teach a rough society the virtues of dependence upon divine grace; one of the richest of sources of medieval folk-lore—folk music, folk motif, folkways and even to some extent, folk speech; and an important aid to the unravelling of Spanish history. Nor would the list of enthusiastic plaudits end here if there were space or need to expand it.

In the production of the *Cantigas de Santa María,* Alfonso was again following an ancient and venerable tradition, this time the gathering of miracles of the Blessed Virgin. Collections in Latin had appeared earlier in most of Europe, and collections in the vernaculars had become common by the twelfth and thirteenth centuries. In Spain, for example, the contemporary *Liber Mariae* of Gil de Zamora had appeared in Latin, and the already mentioned *Milagros de Nuestra Señora* of Berceo in Spanish. Like Berceo, by the way, Alfonso X represented living and practicing devotion to the Virgin. When the king rode into battle, her image went with him attached to his saddle; he bestowed goodly sums upon various of her shrines, and even went so far as to champion her miracles over those of St. James himself, Spain's patron saint.[1] Alfonso, like Berceo, dubbed himself the Virgin's troubadour. He wrote (and I translate):

> And I desire to sing the praise
> of the Virgin, the Mother of Our Lord,
> Holy Mary, who is the best
> thing that He created; and therefore I
> wish to be evermore her troubadour,
> and I beseech her to desire me for her
>
> Troubadour and to wish my singing
> to receive, because in it I wish to reveal
> the miracles which she wrought; (Prologue B, vv. 15–23)

> (*E o que quero é dezir loor*
> *da Virgen, Madre de nostro Sennor,*
> *Santa Maria, que ést' a mellor*
> *cousa que el faz; et por aquest' eu*
> *quero seer oy mais seu trobador,*
> *e rogo-lle que me queira por seu*
>
> *Trobador e que queira meu trobar*
> *reçeber, ca per el quer' eu mostrar*
> *dos miragres que ela fez; . . .*)[2]

It would be interesting to know just when Alfonso began his *Cantigas,* or the planning for their assembling. In 1257, which many scholars believe is the date of completion of the first one hundred of the miracles, the King was in his thirty-sixth year and in the fifth of his reign. The work of gathering, editing, and actually setting down in writing may have started much earlier. We do know, at least, when this work ended, for the entire corpus of over four hundred *cantigas,* representing the definitive edition, was finished either in, or just prior to, 1279.[3] If one is willing to accept the beginning date of 1257, Alfonso by 1279, had been intermittently or steadily at work on the *Cantigas* for nearly a quarter of a century. Probably he started before 1257, for the very mechanics of producing one hundred of these canticles, replete with musical notation, illustrative miniatures, and carefully penned in the excellent and demanding calligraphy of the age undoubtedly required many months, and even years. It is logical to think that Alfonso started on this masterpiece before 1257 for other reasons. One of these is the close personal association between the content of some of the songs and his own life. Some twenty-eight refer either to the King himself, to members of his family, or to people who lived at his court. And of these, several treat happenings which took place when he was very young or even before he was born. One such miracle (222) tells that his father, Ferdinand, while still a small boy, was cured by the Virgin while King Alfonso VIII, Ferdinand's father, was warring in Gascony against England's Henry II. Another (256) is told about the miraculous healing of Alfonso's mother, Queen Beatriz, when Alfonso was six years old. Is it not easy to conjecture that Alfonso might have listened to these miracles at his mother's or his father's knee, or have had them from the mouths of relatives or servitors? They are not found in the chroniclers or elsewhere and would be lost but for the *Cantigas*. Certainly they are reminiscent of the kind of anecdotes in family repertories. It is not at all unlikely, then, in fact it is quite probable, that Alfonso may have been collecting miracles of the Virgin long before the first one hundred appeared in a volume of the *Cantigas de Santa María*.

In the past, possibly owing to that scholarly reticence which leads the expert to avoid making statements as to the authorship of medieval works, some writers hesitated to attribute the composition of the *Cantigas* to the King's personal creativity. Of late, and after careful consideration of content and manner of presentation, medievalists are admitting that he possibly, and even probably, was the author and composer, of many, if not all. *Trobar*, "the composing of lyrical pieces in verse according to the art of the troubadours," was regarded in Alfonso's time as the highest expression of literary genius. Most gentlemen and nobles wrote songs, not all with poetic excellence, but at least with true zeal. Recall the two thousand songs mentioned in Chapter 3, and the fact that these are the production of two hundred definitely known and named poets. Recall, too, that this kind of gentlemanly activity continued into the fourteenth and fifteenth centuries, resulting in even vaster *cancioneros* which also contain the personal creations of kings and princes. Alfonso, known and

esteemed for his erudition, would not have avoided the composition of songs, and it is safe to believe that he composed a considerable portion of the *Cantigas de Santa María.* Moreover, in
the Prologue to the *Cantigas,* written in the first person, as are
some of the *cantigas* themselves, we read:

> Since the writing of verse is an art
> which entails deep understanding,
> a troubadour, therefore,
> should be endowed with this virtue
> and enough powers of reason
> to be able to understand
> that which he wishes to say
> and then come to express it well,
> for good songs are made this way.
>
> While my own poems are perhaps ill-planned
> in some points, still I propose to expand
> upon a thing or two I do know, and,
> through powers such as I have been conferred,
> may God, the Source of Knowledge, stand
> me in good stead (oh poet, hear his word).
>
> (*Porque trobar é cousa en que jaz*
> *entendimento, por en queno faz*
> *á-o d'aver e de razon assaz,*
> *per que entenda e sábia dizer*
> *e que entend' e de dizer lle praz,*
> *ca ben trobar assi s'á de ffazer.*
>
> *E macar eu estas duas non ey*
> *com'eu querria, pero provarei*
> *a mostrar ende un pouca que sei,*
> *confiand' en Deus, ond' o saber ven,*
> *ca per ele tenno que poderei*
> *mostrar do que quero algūa ren.*)   (*Prologo,* vv. 1–12)

These lines show not only that Alfonso wrote them in the first
person, but reveal also the mental equipment and skills required
for *ben trobar,* "excellent troubadour style."
Perhaps the entire vast body of the *Cantigas de Santa María*
may be too much to attribute to one busy king, and perhaps it

is too varied in meters; perhaps, too, the fact that some of the miracles about Alfonso are told in the third person could lead to the belief that he was not their composer; but the number which are written in the first person should not be denied his authorship. Could some professional poet in the King's service have described Alfonso's own emotions and actions so effectively in the first person? In the Learned King's case this hypothesis can hardly be accepted. Besides, there is still more evidence of Alfonso's personal hand in the *Cantigas*, for he is portrayed again and again in the miniatures. Now medievalists know that the appearance of a king's picture in the preface of a book he sponsored is a common occurrence; but it is uncommon, and even rare, for a monarch to be portrayed with frequency, caught almost photographically, as it were, by the artists who depict him engaged in a variety of activities. In number 142, for instance, we see the king mounted on a mule watching his hawks bring down herons. In number 169 the King tells as a first-person account the story of a church in the Moorish quarter of Murcia, the city which he conquered before his coronation. The miniatures reveal him as a prince receiving the Moorish delegation, and later as a king. A few lines of this *cantiga* will suffice to show the personal tone of the story itself:

> And of that I will relate a great miracle, which I saw
> after God gave me Murcia, and which I heard
> many Moors tell who dwelt there previously
> and held the land due to our sinning, . . .
>
> (*E daquest' un miragre direi grande, que vi*
> *des que mi Deus deu Murça, e oý outrossi*
> *dezir a muitos mouros que moravan ant' y*
> *e tīian a terra por nossa pecadilla, . . .*) (*cantiga* 169, vv. 8–11)

It is as though Alfonso were writing a report about his rule in Murcia. Nothing could be more personal.

This intimacy of the King's life in the *Cantigas* is one that has no parallel in other collections of miracles. The importance of such a presentation is quickly apparent. It is responsible for unexpected details and bits of information which historians have found invaluable in dating events of Alfonso's reign. The noted scholar, Evelyn Proctor, who has studied the *Cantigas* from the historian's point of view, makes this quite clear. In discussing number 235, which relates a miracle that saved Alfonso's life when he lay dying in Valladolid, she writes: ". . . it might more justly be described as the king's complaint of the treachery of his nobles and his own difficulties, disappointments, and illnesses, for it is only after a long catalogue of woes and in the seventeenth stanza that we reach the king's illness at Valladolid. Every incident given can be identified and dated, and the poem provides an historical epitome from 1272 to 1278." [4]

The intimacy is responsible likewise for what must have been a strong bond of rapport between the King and various elements among his people—within the middle and lower classes, and the nobility. Since the miracles and hymns were probably sung in the churches, as well as in the royal chapel, at court, and possibly in public places during festivals, many common people must have heard them and, thus, these songs would have served to bring the King closer to the commoner. And the fact that even the lowliest peasant might be the protagonist in a *cantiga* added to this bond of rapport.

Alfonso, then, was deeply involved in the *Cantigas de Santa María* during most of the period of his reign. He seems to have composed a good many of the songs, or, as some believe, all of them. He thought highly enough of these miracles to have a volume of them prepared and presented to his cousin, Louis IX of France. The possibility of Alfonso's direct participation should not be overlooked because it makes the *Cantigas de Santa María* his most intimate and truly creative literary production.

II *The Manuscripts of the* Cantigas

According to the definitive edition of Walter Mettmann, there are four hundred and twenty-seven *cantigas* written to honor the Blessed Virgin, or to relate the miracles she performed for her devotees. Of these, however, only two hundred and seventy-three are actual miracle stories and, therefore, real brief narratives. The rest are *Cantigas de loor*, "songs of praise," which sing her glories, laud her virtues, or stress her beneficence. They are distributed throughout the text at more or less regular intervals. The first appears directly after the King's Prologue, which is also, as we have seen, a piece of lyric verse. Then each tenth *cantiga* throughout the repertoire of miracles is a *cantiga de loor*. Furthermore, in the last one hundred *cantigas* only numbers 404, 405, 407, and 408 are miracles, for the rest are simply hymns to Our Lady and could better be relegated to a history of hymnology and song. So much for the actual number and classification of the *cantigas*.

Four manuscripts[5] of the *Cantigas de Santa María* have survived and may be described as follows: Codex j.b.2 of the Escorial, the largest of all and the one which contains forty miniatures revealing musicians playing their instruments; Escorial T.j.I, the most lavishly illustrated with full-page miniatures numbering over one hundred; Biblioteca Nacional 10069, more often referred to as *To*, signifying Toledo, since it originally belonged to the Cathedral Library at Toledo; and MS Banco Rari of the Biblioteca Nazionale of Florence, formerly known as II. I. 213, also illustrated with beautiful miniatures. A very complete description of these can be found in the edition of Walter Mettmann, cited previously. This edition, incidently, supersedes that of the Marqués de Valmar, published in 1889 with a lengthy and very valuable study by Mussafia.[6]

III *The Language of the* Cantigas

The particular variety, or rather the level, of Galician-Portuguese found in the *Cantigas de Santa María,* follows that erudite development designed by the troubadours as the vehicle of their professional versifying. As mentioned earlier, the troubadours of Spain, whether native speakers of Galician or Spaniards from some other area, employed for their lyrics a dialect of Portuguese spoken in Galicia. So had the troubadours of France preferred the language of Provence. Castilian, Leónese, and Aragonese poets considered it preferable to write in Galician, in their opinion a softer and more apt language for lyric verse. This Galician was not the highly flexible and mature vehicle that Portuguese would become in later ages, but it was, owing to its contacts with Provençal and Catalan, a language of cultural status. It was, then, a Galician refined by poets into a literary medium; it contained the vocabulary of courtly love and, since it was modeled upon the poetry of the Provençal singers, it had turns of phrase and even some syntactical elements not truly native. In spite of this artificiality of phrase and word, however, the language of the Spanish troubadours retained something of its own popular flavor and could be understood by the people to whom the songs were sung, whether they were Galicians or not. It was a Portuguese dialect, admittedly, and people who knew any dialect of Portuguese could understand it. And, since Spaniards were able to understand Portuguese, the language of Old Galicia offered no linguistic problems of moment. Old Spanish and Old Portuguese, even Old Galician, were all in the same stage of development, and contained many similarities not found in their counterparts today. All in all, Galician was a very apt vehicle for troubadour poetry in the Iberian Peninsula. Spanish and Portuguese lyric poets would not relinquish it in favor of pure Portuguese or Spanish for some two hundred years past Alfonso's time.

In employing Galician in the *Cantigas de Santa María*, Alfonso may have actually created a new genre represented solely by this single literary work. For lack of a better name, Martín de Riquer has called it the *canción sacra gallego-portuguesa*, "sacred Galician-Portuguese song." [7] Only the *Cantigas de Santa María* sing in sacred verse the glories of the Virgin and of divine love; the other *cancioneros* offer material of a different tone, indeed, and their very philosophy is far removed from Alfonso's in his *Cantigas*. Three varieties of troubadour verse are usually listed. In the *cantiga de amor* the poet sings of his profane love for a lady who has stolen his heart and who has literally enslaved him. Such poetry is an adaptation of the Provençal *cansó*, and like its model it is conventional, rhetorical, and burdened by the details of the lover's vassalage to his haughty lady whom he addresses as *mia senhor*. The second variety of Galician troubadour poetry is known as the *cantiga de amigo*. In this a lovelorn lass sighs for her absent *amigo*, "lover." Sometimes he is present, and she beseeches him to reciprocate her amorous passion. This is a more primitive kind of verse and is, therefore, even in the conventional versification of the troubadours, fresher and more delightful. After all, it sprang from pure native folksong, recognized by experts as something common to all peoples close to the soil, and is represented in those *jarchas* of the Mozarabs in Andalusia mentioned in Chapter 3. The last of the varieties of the troubadour's poetry is the *cantiga de escarnio* or *de mal dizir*, "song of mockery" or "libel," in which the poet attacks institutions he dislikes or slanders his enemies, both male and female, in terms often so obscene that medieval legislative action was taken against those who offended too greatly in their verses.[8]

Only the Learned King, it seems, used Galician-Portuguese for sacred song; but even though he did so, he strayed far from the rules of formal troubadour poetry, at least in some of his *cantigas*. The very content of the *Cantigas de Santa María* demanded this. The miracles, directed toward all classes of society, even toward members of the lowest levels, are simple and naïve accounts of the Virgin's wonder-working powers. Such an approach was the best, if the songs were to be relished and understood by untutored folk. A large proportion of troubadouresque formality, rhetoric, and conventionality had to be omitted. The words of a peasant woman as she beseeches the Virgin to remove the head of barley that has penetrated her child's body could hardly be set into the formal phraseology of the troubadours (*cantiga* 315). And how could conventional verse become the vehicle of a miracle relating the death of a dragon whose blood, spewed out upon its killer, infects him with leprosy (189)? No, Alfonso did not always abide by the poetic models he chose as the medium for his miracles, although in the case of the *cantigas de loor*, he was more successful in following such rules. When he used Galician-Portuguese, he was simply employing the only poetic medium then considered worthy of literary art. Those who had, a century earlier, written saints' lives had employed the meter of the *mester de juglaría* of the epic poets because that was the medium then esteemed as the best for literature.

The newness of the genre Alfonso created lay, not in its adherence to the conventions and forms of the Galician-Portuguese troubadours, although adherence was there; nor did this newness lie in the popular and folkloristic content of the *Cantigas*, for miracles in Spain had for decades, even centuries, been the subject of popular poetic treatment. It was rather a strange, new, and surprisingly successful blending of erudite forms and meters with popular, pious, intimate, and informal subject matter. If one could visualize a folk ballad set into the poetic measures of an

Italian sonnet, he might draw a reasonably well-defined conception of what Alfonso had achieved in the *Cantigas de Santa María*.

IV *The Subject Matter and the Sources of the* Cantigas

Classifications of the subject matter of the *Cantigas* have been
prepared by scholars but none is definitive, and few are even
adequate, for the vastness and the variety of the miracles is too
great to permit completeness in either of these areas of investigation. Calcott and Bell, the Marqués de Valmar, and Mussafia have
attempted to classify the themes and motifs, the last to a greater
extent. So has Valbuena Prat, although in a much more general
way.[9] The present writer has nearly finished the rather onerous
task of preparing a motif-index of the *cantigas* made in accordance with the world-standard index of Stith Thompson. I have
found that from the viewpoint of thematology classification may
simply not be feasible or perhaps even possible.

The same lack of completeness can be seen in source studies
of these miracles. Some sources, it is true, can be identified and
even proved; for example, the already alluded to miracles concerning the life of Alfonso, members of his family or his friends.
Others can be no more than surmised; many simply cannot be
traced; this is especially true of scores of motifs which are derived
from the folklore of the people. The subject matter of the *Cantigas* is not limited to Iberia. Alfonso's Suabian mother brought
with her when she came to Spain to marry King Ferdinand a
Germanic retinue made up most probably of noblemen and ladies
in waiting, cooks, butlers, chamberlains, dressmakers, physicians,
poets, and artists. Such people would have brought with them,
along with their language and culture, a store of popular German
lore and folkways among which would surely have been found
accounts of miracles. One can hazard the guess that at least one
of the *Cantigas de Santa María* came to Alfonso from some member of this transplanted German court, or perhaps Queen Beatriz
herself related it to her son. *Cantiga* 74 is entitled *Como Santa
Maria guareceu o pintor que o demo quisera matar porque o
pintava feo* ("How Holy Mary protected the painter whom the
demon wished to slay because he painted him ugly"). It might
well have originated in Germany from a proverb well-known to

this day in that country, but not found in the repositories of Spanish maxims. This German proverb translated into English is, "Never paint the devil on a wall," a thing that the painter in the *cantiga* did with frightful results. It is likely that in Germany the proverb gave rise to the miracle, or that, in reverse, the miracle might have given rise to the proverb, for either could have been the parent of the other. It is quite possible, then, that the miracle came from Germany fully developed, and that it quickly made its way into the growing Alfonsine repertoire. If so, a bit of Germanic lore helped to shape one of the *Cantigas*.

Some miracles of a nonliterary category might well have come from other foreign languages, for Alfonso's court swarmed with writers and artistic people from far and wide—France, England, Italy, Portugal, Byzantium, Moorish Spain, and Islamic lands beyond the sea. Delegations came occasionally from as far off as Egypt. One such mission deserves special mention, as it is definitely connected with the *Cantigas*. The *Crónica de los Reyes de Castilla*, "Chronicle of the Kings of Castile," Chapter IX, reports that each year on the anniversary of the death of King Ferdinand, delegations came to Seville to honor the King.[10] One was sent by the Sultan of Egypt, Alvandexaver. "And they brought presents to this King Don Alfonso of many fabrics, priceless, and of diverse natures, and many jewels, rich and exotic. And they brought likewise an elephant and an animal which they call *azorafa*, and an ass which was striped, for it had a white band and then another one black, and they brought other beasts and animals of many kinds." A delightful parallel to this account in the chronicle is to be found in the *Cantigas de Santa María*, for in one of the songs of praise (29) we see the strange beasts kneeling to Our Lady. The *azorafa* is, as might be expected, a giraffe, which can be seen in the miniature so correctly depicted that there can be no doubt that the artist used a living animal as a model. The elephant is also there, and the "ass with stripes," as well as a camel and what may be a gnu. Visible also is either a rhinoceros or hippopotamus, half-concealed behind the other mammals. Sundry exotic birds complete the group of worshipful creatures, and among these are an Egyptian ibis and flamingoes.

Incidentally, the aforementioned chronicle states on the same page that the king of Granada also sent delegations to honor the

Learned King's father, offering additional proof of the close ties existing between Moslem and Christian Spain. The influence of Moorish story upon the *Cantigas* can only be surmised, but it can be stated with certainty that many *cantigas* described Moslem activities in Alfonso's time and in the centuries before him.

A few of the definitely known sources were the richly illustrated *Miracles de la Sainte Vierge,* "Miracles of the Holy Virgin," of Gautier de Coincy; the *Speculum Historiale,* "Mirror of History," of Vincent de Beauvais, a copy of which, according to the chronicles, was actually sent to Alfonso by the king of France, for Alfonso mentions this fact in his last will and testament; the *De Miraculis Beatae Mariae Virginis,* "Of the Miracles of the Blessed Virgin Mary," of unknown authorship; the *Liber Mariae,* "Book of Mary," of Gil de Zamora, who seems to have assisted the Learned King in the writing of some of his histories: the *De Miraculis Beatae Virginis Mariae* of Walter of Cluny; the *Scala Coeli,* "Ladder of Heaven," of Johannes Gobius; the *Liber Miraculis Sanctae Mariae Dei Genetrix,* "The Book of St. Mary, the Mother of God," possibly composed by Patho; the *Mariale Magnum,* "Greatness of Mary," attributed without authority to St. Isidore of Seville; and most probably the *Milagros de Nuestra Señora* of Gonzalo de Berceo.

The Marqués de Valmar suggests many other themes of foreign origin, as does Mussafia.[11] I have mentioned in several articles Alfonso's debt to various collections of miracles and to folklore.[12] I might repeat here a few of the more pertinent of these observations from an article in *The Southern Folklore Quarterly.* Some of the miracles resemble stories from Holy Scripture, although they have been reworked and greatly altered, with new characters and new settings. *Cantiga* 241 is an excellent example. A young man, during the festivities of his wedding day, lost his balance and fell several stories to the street. Mortally wounded, he was carried to the shrine of the Virgin where he was completely and instantaneously healed. The tale parallels that of Eutychus in Acts 20: 9–12; Eutychus fell from a window and was resuscitated by St. Paul. Another of this type is *cantiga* 143 in which a merchant is bound hand and foot and cast overboard by sailors who dislike him. They tie the other end of the rope to the vessel's side so as to be able to retrieve the body and report the man's death as an accidental drowning. Three days later they haul the body aboard, only to find that he has not died. The Virgin had caused a bubble to form around him. Similarities between this story and that of Jonah are obvious.

In the same article I pointed out that earlier pieces of medieval literature furnished Alfonso with material for his *Cantigas*. Number 98 is the story of an invisible force which prevented the entry of a sinful woman into the church at Valverde, a tale quite reminiscent of one of the events in the life of St. Mary the Egyptian, mentioned in Chapter 3. And there is the *cantiga* (103) about a monk who listened to the song of a little bird while three centuries passed.

Now all the *cantigas* discussed thus far, save that of the exotic animals, have appeared in some collection of miracles either in Latin, in a vernacular tongue, or in the Bible. Others, however, must be attributed to folklore in Spain and these, of course, are not to be found in other collections of the Virgin's miracles. Take, for example, the story of Marisaltos, Jewess of Segovia, as treated in *cantiga* 107. Condemned to death by her people because she has become a Christian convert, she is cast down from a cliff, but is saved by the Virgin who brings her safely to earth. This miracle is still told in Spain and Spanish America. The miniature depicts these events, as does a fresco painting on the wall of the cloister of Segovia's Cathedral. This is an instance, then, of a local folk legend.

Other *cantigas* are very much a part of local lore, too. Such erudite collectors as Gautier de Coincy used no such miracles, but Alfonso, who realized the rapport to be had with his people by including miraculous occurrences which many of them had witnessed or heard about, added stories of this variety. One tells of a woman who believed that a serpent had entered her body and was alive in her stomach. The Virgin at the Shrine of Our Lady of Porto told her to go to Cadiz and pray at the Cathedral, which she straightway did. After the prayer had been said, the woman vomited up a red snake. I have heard a similar folk tale in Kentucky from a mountain woman minus, of course, the Virgin's aid and the Spanish setting. Number 18 sings of some remarkable silkworms in Segovia which wove two lengths of silk cloth to be used in robes for the Virgin's image. A furrier (49) so as to leave his hands free to work, placed a needle between his lips and teeth. It became lodged in his throat and he was in agony for days until he dragged himself to the shrine of Our Lady to pray and be cured. Many more miracles of folkloristic background occur in the *Cantigas,* but few have been studied. When more of the autochthonous aspects of these songs have been examined, our knowledge of the Spanish Middle Ages in the areas of belief, tale, folk medicine, folk music and folk arts and crafts will be vastly broadened.

A few words, too, should be devoted to the contribution of the *Cantigas* to our understanding of daily life in the thirteenth century.[13] Here, as in the case of folkloristic elements in the *Cantigas,* there is great wealth of detail. The scenes of many of the miracles were cities and towns and, therefore, the miniatures give a remarkable picture of plazas, streets, alleys, churches, palaces, monasteries and nunneries, private homes, the houses of Jews and Moors, in short, of whole cross-sections of city life. In *cantiga* 4 one sees something rare and quite instructive, for the first panel reveals a schoolroom with a monk, who is the teacher, and students, all of whom are boys. They sit on the floor while the pedagogue explicates a book. Later the pupils go to the chapel for Holy Communion. One, who is a Jew, does not participate, but instead stands before the image of the Virgin while his companions receive the Sacrament. During this time the image of Our Lady extends her hand from the altar and gives the young Jew a holy wafer. At home—and here again we are privileged to see an unusual sight—the Jewish father, a glassmaker, rebukes his son and casts the lad into the heated glass-furnace from which he is saved by the Virgin. This picture of a Jewish home and glass factory is one of great value. The event, by the way, took place, according to the *cantiga,* in Canterbury.

Cantiga 25 opens to the eye of the reader the establishment of a moneychanger; 28 shows a city under attack by the Moors with siege machinery, men in armor and many of the weapons of war; 34 is the story of a Jew who threw a portrait of Our Lady into a latrine, thereby depicting just what these facilities were like; number 13 gives all the details of a medieval execution by hanging from a tree, while in number 175 a youth hangs from a man-made gallows; something closely resembling a baseball game appears in 42; and a thirteenth-century variety of bullfight can be studied in 144.

Rural scenes are quite plentiful as are seascapes, with many varieties of civilian and military crafts. Pilgrimages are depicted, dances, funerals, cavalry battles, infantry attacks, Moorish incursions—a mighty panorama of life as it was lived by medieval man.

One last matter should be mentioned in connection with the *Cantigas,* and this is their subjectivity, their deep consciousness of environment and of people, and especially of the latter's reaction to environment. Américo Castro, one of the greatest and most controversial Spanish scholars of modern times, believes that this subjectivity and personal reaction to physical surroundings is a product of the quasioriental, quasioccidental culture of Spain, and that without the Moors the *Cantigas* (and for that matter many other monuments of Spanish literature), could not have been written. To support this phenomenon in the *Cantigas* he compares the objective treatment of the *cantiga* used by Gautier de Coincy with the "Hispano-Islamic" handling of it in the *Cantigas de Santa María.* His point is well taken, although many of the most outstanding scholars today will have none of Castro's suggestions.[14]

When all the miniatures in the three codices containing them have been studied in their entirety, scholars will be able to understand more clearly the way of life and the thought of their medieval ancestors.

V *Versification of the* Cantigas

In turning to the versification of the *Cantigas,* one should recall two important facts. They are true songs with full musical notation and were certainly intended to be sung in the Spanish churches, probably at court and at gatherings of the aristocracy, and possibly in the public square or in the country—wherever celebrations of the feasts of the Virgin were held. The second fact is this: Alfonso used as the basis for his *cantigas* an erudite poetry devised by the troubadours of Galicia who had modeled their own art upon the poetic conventions of Provence. We have mentioned that in the miracles, which are narratives in verse, the king and his poets wandered somewhat far afield from the troubadouresque rules and patterns, but that in the *cantigas de loor,* or songs of praise, they made greater efforts to conform to poetic regulations. In these hymns, then, the King followed the troubadour tradition in which the poet sang the adoration and high praises of the earthly lady who possessed his heart and soul. This poetry of the troubadours in Provence and France and in Portugal, Galicia and the rest of Spain, reflected the philosophy of courtly love which in the twelfth, and to a smaller degree in the thirteenth century, had been in great vogue in much of Western Europe, and which would linger on in the Iberian Peninsula, to remain in popularity until well into the fifteenth century.

Alfonso, instead of lauding the physical, amatory, and other charms of a mortal woman, sang in his sacred *cantigas* the praises of Our Lady, and in a spirit of gratitude, deep respect and spiritual love, related her miracles. He regarded her, and not some earthly lady, in his songs as the exemplification of the perfect qualities of womanhood. If an amorous tone occasionally obtains in his hymns and miracles, it is but a reflection of the troubadour school of poetry under whose rules he wrote.

It is to Dorothy Clotelle Clarke of the University of California that we owe a truly masterly article on the versification of the *Cantigas* of Alfonso.[15] She writes of the wide range of meters found in these songs and of the remarkable fact that in them one finds possible sources for all Spanish meters. "That is to say that Alfonso's ability," she writes, "to select, at almost the very dawn of Peninsular formal poetry, lasting qualities in so intricate an art as that of versification is indeed admirable. All presently known verse forms employed in Castilian before the Golden Age are found in the *Cantigas*. And there is in the collection a foreshadowing, as Menéndez y Pelayo indicates, of the Golden Age and modern times. Alfonso's system of verse measure—syllable count—was the one followed almost exactly in subsequent Castilian poetry. Alfonso's rhythmic patterns have lived to the present time and his strophe forms could have been prototypes for a number of basic Castilian strophes. His great fondness for polymetric combinations is of particular significance." An equal amount of originality in musical notation and melody, closely connected, of course, to versification will be examined briefly in the section of this chapter devoted to the music of the *Cantigas*.

The most frequently used poetic form in the *Cantigas* was the *zéjel,*[16] of Arabic origin according to some or, as others believe, of Mozarab precedence, and borrowed by the Arabic poets of Andalusia from their Christian subjects. But the form is known to have appeared also in Hebrew and Christian liturgies, and parallels exist in the Franco-Provençal *virelai,* the Catalonian *goig* and the Castilian *villancico.* In a typical *zéjel* the thematic refrain, called in Spanish the *estribillo,* is repeated before each strophe. In the *Cantigas* the *estribillo* may contain two or more verses, for greater variety in this aspect is permitted. Even the lines themselves vary greatly from two syllables (*cantiga* 276) to seventeen (*cantiga* 5), but the favorite was the octosyllable, perhaps the most popular of all even in Spain today. Gilbert Chase mentions two *estribillos* that were very much used. "Many of them consist of four-line stanzas (rhyme scheme, BBBA), with a refrain in the form of a rhymed couplet (AA) coming before and after each stanza. Others have a four-line refrain (ABAB) and a six-line stanza with alternating rhyme." [17]

A typical example of a long-lined *estribillo* (*cantiga* 5) must be seen in the original language, if it is to be properly understood and its metrification savored:

> *Quena coitas deste mundo ben quiser soffrer,*
> *Santa Maria deve sempr' antesi põer.*
> (Who wishes to endure the cares of this world
> ought ever to place Holy Mary before him.)

And a shorter *estribillo* is that found in *cantiga* 11:

> *Macar ome per folia*
> *aginna caer*
> *pod' en pecado*
> *do ben de Santa Maria*
> *non dev' a seer*
> *desesperado.* (vv. 1–6)
> (Although a man through folly
> is able to fall
> into sinfulness,
> he should not despair
> of the goodness
> of Holy Mary.)

Dorothy Clarke shows that variations in the *zéjel* are indeed numerous and include alternating rhyme which replaces the monorhymed sequences. Sometimes other rhymes are inserted between the original monorhymed lines: *abababac, dededec* (numbers 156, 157, 180). Some use longer monorhymed sequences (95, 283), and there are some in which there is the insertion of an extra rhyme between two lines having consonant rhyme: *aaabab, cccbcb* (239). She refers to a variety of other examples.

"Among the strophes less popular with Alfonso el Sabio in the *Cantigas*," she goes on to say, "but which became strophes of primary importance in Castilian are: the *redondilla*—though not octosyllabic in the *Cantigas* (Nos. 230, 326, p. 589); the *pareado* (No. 260); the *copla de pie quebrado* (No. 300); monorhymed quatrains similar to the *cuaderna vía* strophe but having different lines (p. 599); a form closely resembling the *romancillo* (No. 401); and above all, a *romance* (No. 308)." This *romance* is the earliest version of this form that she had found in the poetry of the Iberian Peninsula.

In a typical *zéjel*, as has been mentioned above, the last verse in the *estribillo* sets the pattern of rhyme for the last verse in the strophe. In *cantiga* 14 this is well represented. For convenience I have italicized the last word in the *estribillo* and the last word in the following strophe.

> Con razon é d' averen gran pavor
> as bestias da Madre daquel Sennor
> que sobre todas cousas á *poder*.
>
> E dest' un gran miragre foi mostrar
> Santa Maria, a Virgen sen par,
> en Prazença, per com' oý contar
> a omees bõos et de *creer*. (vv. 3–9)
>
> (With reason wild beasts fear the
> Mother of that Master who
> has power over all things.
>
> And about this a great miracle
> Holy Mary, the Virgin without peer,
> revealed in Placencia, as I hear,
> to good and faith-filled men.)

Dr. Clarke discusses a great many other metrical forms of importance, not all of which can be given here. She states that the hendecasyllable is most important, and then the heptasyllable, although the former was not the same form as the Italianate made famous later by Boscán and Garcilaso. She shows examples of twelve-syllable lines (*cantigas* 123, 145, 209, and 223) and of fourteen in *cantiga* 16; and she reveals that canticle 240 has a rare accent on the fourth syllable, while 211 is accented consistently on the fifth; occasionally the pattern varies within a given poem. An example of something closely resembling the *arte mayor* current in the fifteenth century is to be seen, she says, in numbers 79 and 307, for example—the only difference between the form as used by Alfonso and the later writers being the regularity of syllable count in the former. Nine- and thirteen-syllable lines, not known in Castilian until the late nineteenth century, appear in the *Cantigas* (25 and 73), she also reveals.

"The shortest line used as the sole verse-length in a poem," she proves, "is the hexasyllable, which appears in both the patterns later found in Castilian, particularly during and after the Golden Age: the *serranilla* (No. 192) having fluctuating secondary accent: . . ." She goes on to indicate that there are examples of the decasyllable (*cantigas* 15, 20, and 280), the fourteen-syllable (12, 23, and others), and the fifteen-syllable (36).

Among her other discoveries is what appears to be a perfect *romancillo* (420) of the type much in vogue in the Golden Age.

The rhyme itself of the *Cantigas* is pure consonance—not assonance—with an almost perfect rhyme pattern, for a pattern set down in the first strophe is faithfully continued in all the other strophes. And the rhyme scheme, too, is rich in variety.

Some who read the songs of Alfonso X find a few which appear to be unartistically written. As will be pointed out in section six of this chapter, which is devoted to the music of the *Cantigas*, so close are the ties between the poems and the music that what appears to be a lack of artistry disappears if one hears the music as he reads the words. Excellent musical recordings have been prepared in recent years, and these are listed in the Bibliography.

Perhaps the thoughts of Menéndez y Pelayo on the *Cantigas de Santa María* are the most cogent and valuable that can be used to indicate in a general way the value and importance of Alfonsine versification. This great Spanish scholar early in his career studied the *Cantigas* and recognized them for the remarkable heritage they hold in store. "But the *Cantigas*," he wrote, and I translate, "not only are important for their linguistic value and for their hagiographical content, but for the extraordinary variety and relative perfection of their metrical forms. They are, taken as a whole, the oldest manifestation known until this day in any of the Literatures of the Peninsula, and not very posterior to the few remains which we have of Castilian epic meter." [18]

VI *The Music of the* Cantigas

No student of musicology, I can only avail myself of the expert knowledge of those who do know the area. With their aid I have prepared the following brief synthesis of the music of the *Cantigas*.

Gilbert Chase, in his well-known study of Spanish music, said: "It is known that Spanish kings and nobles employed Moorish-Arabian musicians in their palaces. Some of the miniatures of the *Cantigas* of Alfonso the Wise of Castile, for example, show Moorish musicians playing various instruments together with Spanish musicians." [19]

Certainly, Alfonso, a musician himself, imported, as was the custom of medieval royalty, many jongleurs and troubadours from Europe as well as many musicians from Moorish Spain and probably North Africa. Gilbert Chase discusses one of the miniatures in which the king is seen with his scribes and musicians. Another miniature comes to mind in support of Chase's observations. This is one of the canticles of praise entitled *Esta e a primeira cantiga de loor de Santa Maria ementando os VII goyos que ouve de seu fillo*, "This is the First Song of Praise of Holy Mary Showing the Seven Joys which She Had from her Son," in ms. T.j.I. The King sits in the center of the picture and turns the pages of a book which rests upon a writing desk at his side. He points, as a teacher might, and seems to be explaining what is in the book. At his left, sitting on the floor, is a scribe who is a priest, as is indicated by his tonsure; at the King's right sits another scribe or secretary, who may be a layman. Both hold open books, and one may see on their pages the words of a song and the lines of the musical score ready for the notes. At the far right of the miniature stand three clerics. One holds a book and the others, looking at it, are in the act of singing. To the far left three musicians, tuning their viols, stand awaiting the king's command. Here, as in the case of the miniature cited by Chase, we may have an example of the actual "trying out" of a *cantiga*. From what is depicted it would seem that Alfonso has just dictated a song to his scribes and that the three singers are practicing it, while the three musicians wait their turn to give it instrumental interpretation.

Incidentally, it should be recalled, j.b.2 provides a remarkably rich depiction of musicians and instruments. Seventy-odd musicians, both Christian and Moslem, are portrayed playing instruments ranging from a wide variety of the percussion type to the family of the strings (lutes, viols, *vihuelas,* etc.), to organs, the hurdy-gurdy and others. One sees two varieties of guitars—the *guitarra morisca* and the *guitarra latina* as well as the rebec, sets of silver bells and hammers with which to play them, transverse flutes, trumpets of various sorts, harps and bagpipes, castanets, and so on.

The actual melodies of the *cantigas* were drawn, no doubt, from a variety of sources. Some belong to the music of the Church whose liturgies furnished melodies; others are taken from Moorish and Arabic and even Hebrew music; many are songs used by the Galician-Portuguese and Franco-Provençal troubadours; perhaps some were brought by professional musicians, singers, and composers from as far away as Italy, England, and the Germanies. One wonders if some of the Suabian musicians, who could have accompanied Princess Beatriz to Spain when she came to marry King Ferdinand, might not have supplied still others. Perhaps most important and fecund of all was the volume of songs originating with the Spanish people themselves. Regional songs abounded then as they do today, and the songs of many social strata and professions must have also existed: harvest songs of farmers, the songs of shepherds and cowboys, sailors' chanties, soldiers' ballads, watchmen's songs, and hunters' and fishermen's ditties may have all contributed. "The interplay of popular and artistic elements," writes Chase, "has nowhere been more significantly revealed than in Spanish music."

When after centuries of oblivion the *Cantigas* were studied at

last by nineteenth-century musicologists, they were not understood and therefore were criticized as being of poor musical quality. The same was the fate of the songs of the Provençal and
French troubadours, for no one could appreciate their true beauty
which was concealed behind a system of musical notation not
properly deciphered. Ribera in Spain had tried to prove that the
Cantigas, as well as other Spanish lyrical pieces, stemmed from
Arabic music, and although this may be considered in a small
part true, in that Arabic melodies were doubtless taken into the
Cantigas, the notation, even of these, is western.[20] The person
who finally managed to decipher the system of notation used by
the thirteenth-century scribes at Alfonso's court is Higinio Anglés,
perhaps Spain's greatest musicologist. I translate: "The repertory
of the four hundred and twenty-three *Cantigas de Santa María,*"
he writes, "as presented in the extant texts, is to the present time,
the most important repertory in Europe as regards medieval
sacred lyric. The melodies have no relationship at all with the
oriental music of the Arabs. . . . The notation of the *Cantigas*
. . . is most perfect, although until very recently it has been
unknown by musicologists." [21]

Apparently many musicians and students of music had studied
the Alfonsine songs, and all had been surprised at their "poor"
quality. But this was owing to the mistaken belief that they
could be studied and translated in accordance with the rules of
musical notation made by modern musicologists. Anglés finally
saw that no established regulations could be followed in the case
of the *Cantigas,* and that it would be necessary to use the original
transcription, as it appeared in the codices, and to develop his
own techniques of understanding and transcribing what the medieval scribe had penned. "Thanks to his form of notation we can
today assert that the Spanish melodies offer a rhythmic variety
and a melodic richness which admit no comparison with other
European repertories," continues Anglés.[22]

Anglés had, alongside his interest in medieval music, a lively
interest in Spanish folk song, in particular, and European folk
song, in general. He gathered and studied hundreds, and found
that modern folk songs and the way they are sung by the folk
performers in the villages and mountains and plains, contain
much of the same melodic richness, and often a good deal of the

form and actual melody, as the canticles in King Alfonso's *Canti-gas de Santa María*. "In them, [the *Cantigas*]," he writes, "the rhythmic element of the folk song rules, as we do not find it in the lyrics of the troubadours and minnesingers. . . . Specialists had believed until recently that medieval monody must have had a close relationship with the polyphony of its epoch, and, since in this polyphony only the ternary measure was practiced, this rhythm alone was possible in the monody. But the notation of the *Cantigas* reveals just the opposite. In them is presented the ter-nary measure which combines with the binary; again melodies exist which can be sung with only the binary." [23]

This discovery of Anglés will eventually have even a more telling effect upon the study of the music of the troubadours, from which so many of the *Cantigas* came. For their music, like the *Cantigas*, had been subjected to the rules of medieval poly-phony, because scholars had believed—and many still do believe—that polyphony was the key to understanding, and obviously this was a mistake in dealing with monody. These specialists had for years sought some manuscript that might offer a clue, or better still, an actual guide to the understanding of monody. "Well then," Anglés tells us, "these manuscripts which we looked for and never found, have just been discovered: they are the Spanish manuscripts of the Court of Castile and León; they are the manu-scripts of the *Cantigas* of Alfonso el Sabio." [24]

Beyond this point in the technical discussion of Anglés, who is the expert acknowledged by musicologists as the best in the field, I cannot go, for this would require the skills of a trained student of the very science of music; however, I can, even as a layman, see, as can any reader, something at least, of the magni-tude of Anglés' work and what it means to the entire study of the medieval lyric. I can also see what his discoveries mean to the case in point, that is, the *Cantigas de Santa María*, all of which definitely points to the native Spanish folkloristic quality of the Alfonsine melodies. [25]

VII *The Pictorial Art of the* Cantigas

One cannot discuss the *Cantigas de Santa María* effectively solely from a literary viewpoint, for the miracles and hymns in the book are inextricably interwoven with the pictorial and musical presentations. Therefore, although no student of medieval art, I must perforce offer at least a general treatment of the artistic qualities of the miniatures, just as I did in the case of the musical notations in Section VI.

The pages of the most lavishly illustrated codex of the *Cantigas,* Escorial T.j.I, are large and measure four hundred and eighty-five millimeters in height by three hundred and twenty-six in width. Each page of miniatures is divided into six panels or compartments, save for one which contains eight, and in each panel some part of the action of that *cantiga* is depicted. The closest modern parallel to these techniques is that used in comic books with their divisions and labels. The labels in the miniatures are captions which appear above each panel in beautiful calligraphy, with the letters in deep blue or brilliant red. The six panels of each page of miniatures are framed together, as though they were a single picture, by a band of designs repeated again and again in brilliant colors, and these designs are believed to take their origin from ceramics and painted sculpture of the period. There is great variety and much artistic excellence in these frames —but more about this particular aspect later. The six-panel division, it should be stated, though carried out in almost every single one of the pages of miniatures, nonetheless does not actually limit the sequences of action to six parts. Some panels are further divided within themselves, with various means employed to accomplish this result. *Cantiga* 9 in the fourth panel shows what at first glance appears to be two monks, the first of whom is facing a lion, the second a group of armed robbers. In actuality the same monk faces lion and robbers, for his two adventures are divided within the panel by a line of trees and mountain slopes. In *cantiga* 64, also in the fourth panel, two entirely different scenes are created by the device of a wall and a column which serve as lines of demarcation.

Sometimes, to add greater dimension to the miniatures, the artists depict characters, either animal or human, beyond the framework of a panel. In describing number 119, Charles Nelson says that "Panel Four is so closely connected with the action of Panel Three that the two can be treated almost as one drawing. These two panels combined are probably the two most outstanding of the *Cantigas* as to related actions, continuity and visualization. The chief demon is shown on the rooftop directing the capture of the High Judge and, at the same moment of time, is shown directing the demons and their disposal of the Judge in Panel Four. . . . This is an astonishingly high level of achievement in the art of animation for the thirteenth century." [26]

I might add that my own observation of number 63 is also pertinent here. In a battle scene which begins in panel three one sees Christian knights charging. The usual band of roseates separates this panel from panel four, but across the line of division, action is continued in an interesting fashion. The rear of a horse is seen in panel three, and the rest of the animal mounted by a knight appears in panel four, as though no line of demarcation were there to prevent its charge. Movement and its continuation are admirably produced here.

Perhaps a good, if not professional, way to arrive at an understanding of the pictorial presentation of the *Cantigas de Santa María* is to choose one set of typical miniatures—one page of the book, that is—and to describe its content. *Cantiga* 157, which can be seen in black-and-white reproduction in an available book, serves conveniently as a point of reference. [27] The border or frieze of design surrounding this particular page of miniatures is, in this case, composed of four-petaled roseates in alternating scarlet and azure on a background ranging from pearl gray to shades of lavender and pink and pale red. The panels, which the eyes are supposed to examine from left to right and from top to bottom, represent a continuum of movement. Those on the left, however, in which the king and his group of companions appear, show little movement, whereas the ones to the right offer scenes of lively action. The alternation of these—the static or near-static scene first, then a scene of action, then another of static reality, and so on until the last—produces quite successfully the concept of fluidity and continuity.

In the first panel Alfonso himself, identified by a plum-colored robe and a hat on which is clearly visible the lion of León, appears against the background of subdued blues worn by his companions and the natural color of the mules and greyhounds. Mules, by the way, at least when one was hunting, were considered in those times as less skittish and safer than horses. Alfonso is portrayed, as he always is in the *Cantigas*, as a rather handsome young man, well proportioned, with a face pleasant and, if not actually plump, at least not thin. His eyes are large and set wide apart. The King has just loosed a falcon upon some herons, and his hand and arm are still raised as the hawk soars upward. In panel two the hawk has wounded a heron which can be seen hurtling toward the surface of the river. Another heron rests on the water, and still a third flies across the sky. The falcon climbs still higher and crosses the borders of the panel to invade the caption, thereby giving a feeling of great dimension and space. In this, we see a nascent impressionism side by side with realism.

The first caption reads: *Como el Rey don Alffonso lançou un falcon a huna garça,* "How King Don Alfonso loosed a falcon upon a heron"; the second caption is this: *Como o falcon firiu a garça e britoull' a ala e caeu a garça no rio,* "How the falcon struck the heron and broke its wing and the heron fell into the river."

Panel three reveals that the King called for a volunteer to retrieve the heron, since the dogs coud not be sent into the turbulent waters. The caption reads: *Como el começou a dezir a vozes quen' entrara pola la garça,* "How he began to call loudly for someone to go in after the heron." His companions here are revealed in fine detail. There are eight mounted men and two footmen, and these latter are holding two greyhounds on leashes.

Panel four is a scene of lively action and violent movement. The caption reads: *Como un omne entrou pola garça e agua o samorgullou ben tres vezes,* "How a man went into the water after the heron and the water drew him down." A hawk sweeps across the sky over the struggle in the river which is bounded by high banks and verdant trees. Two dogs, not greyhounds, but retrievers, watch from the shore on which grow some four separate species of wildflowers. The man, though under the water, can be seen clearly, for the artists have depicted him as though they were peering through glass at his underwater struggles, much as one looks into an aquarium today.

In panel five the caption reads: *Como deu a garça al Rey e el Rey e todos loaron muyto Sancta Maria,* "How he gave the heron to the King and the King and all the others greatly praised Holy Mary." The pictorial action in the miniatures parallels that described in the poetic narration. The man screams and implores the Virgin's aid. The King's companions all cry out that his life is as good as lost; but Alfonso says that Our Lady will not fail to render assistance, and this proves to be true. Panel six shows the man climbing the steep bank, the heron in his hand, and the caption reads: *Como Sancta Maria fez sayr o omne do rio con sa garça na mano,* "How Holy Mary makes the man leave the river with the heron in his hand." Add to this double form of presentation—visual in the miniatures and written in the verses—the added attraction of a musical melody of great beauty, and one can readily see the power of such a threefold presentation to the eye, the ear, and the mind.

Color is not as riotous on this page of miniatures as in some, but its use is equally tasteful and effective. The king's pinkish or plum-colored robe is the focal point in the three perpendicular left-hand panels and attracts the eye to him. The three perpendicular right-hand panels strike a telling contrast with those on the left. The sky and the river are in pastels, it is true, but the river has deeper shades designed to delineate waves. The foliage of the trees and all the grasses and shrubs are dark green; the tiny blossoms are predominantly white. All this surrounded and framed by the brilliantly colored roseates in scarlet and azure produces a delightful over-all presentation, rich, eye-catching, that closely parallels and, therefore, enhances the verbal account.

All the miniatures in this Escorial manuscript, as well as in those of Toledo and Florence, are polychromatic. Shades of red, blue, yellow, green, and brown and black predominate, but pastels abound. Gold illumination is very common, used primarily to set off haloes, royal and celestial crowns, crosses, lamps, altarpieces and the columns of churches; but golden bedsteads, especially those of Alfonso and other royal personages, and tables and doorways are also to be found. Medieval artists were able to obtain striking illuminations by using finely beaten gold-leaf laid over a coating of Armenian bole, a red clay which imparted a very special glow to such work.

It is believed that each miniature was a composite of the work of several, or even of many artists' work. Calligraphers set down the captions; apprentices probably were given the task of drawing and painting the friezes in the frames; and other apprentices may have been allowed to sketch some of the general and conventionalized background scenes. Possibly some of the better artists drew only the first bare charcoal sketches. One can see such beginnings in the Florentine manuscript in which some of the miniatures appear in varying stages of completion. Perhaps after the sketches had been finished, the painters made their contributions. Some of these Florentine miniatures also contain human figures which at first glance seem to be complete; but a closer scrutiny reveals the absence of hands and faces, always difficult to portray. No doubt these awaited the finishing touch of that specialist who could most accurately and skilfully paint them in. The incomplete manuscript, by the way, may be a boon rather than a misfortune, for in it may lie important sectors of the history of medieval miniature production, proving that each page was produced in assembly-line fashion. Dr. Guerrero Lovillo[28] believes that he has identified the style of at least three separate unidentified artists through a careful study of what he thinks are three different manners and techniques of depicting the human body and face. Whether any of these styles is the work of one of three painters whose names have come down to us may never be known, for though three are named in contemporary documents, there is no indication of what part each painter played in any Alfonsine project.

With this general explanation and the description of one of the pages of miniatures presented, other more specific aspects and characteristics can be taken up. Dr. Guerrero Lovillo offers the suggestion that the idea for the depiction and designing of the miniatures may have come from the ivory dyptichs of thirteenth-century France and Spain.[29] These, though no longer possessed of their brilliant coloration, are known from the faded and chipped remains of paint upon them to have been polychromatic. Each is framed by a border of carved roseates or other designs identical to some of those found in the friezes in the *Cantigas*. And each is a sculptural representation of some miracle. Furthermore, each dyptich is divided into six panels, each of which depicts in ivory the events taking place. Other scholars have suggested that stained-glass windows, also portraying miracles, might have served the king and his artists as models when they planned the miniatures. Then, too, since Paris at the time was a center of the art of making miniatures, as attested in Dante's *Paradiso*, the

Alfonsine miniatures may be no more than a hispanization of this French art.

One might even suggest still another inspiration for the artists who created the miniatures for the *Cantigas*. Might not a dramatization of such miracles as could have lent themselves to dramatic presentation have suggested much to the artists? We have seen in Chapter 3 that drama dealing with miracles was common in medieval Europe, both in Latin and in the vernaculars. Could there not have been in Spain dramatizations of some of the Virgin's miracles? After all, in France about 1265 Rutebeuf had produced his *Miracle de Théophile,* "Miracle of Theophilus," in which the Virgin saved the soul of Theophilus who had sold it to the devil. If so much French influence is felt in other Spanish artistic manifestations, why not drama based upon the miracles of Our Lady? The miracle of Theophilus, by the way, is one of those included in the *Cantigas de Santa María.* Nor is it difficult to imagine this miracle acted out in Spain. Indeed, many others might just as easily have been adapted to dramatic form. In so far as I know, however, no one has suggested this possibility. Nor has anyone pointed out, aside from this writer,[30] that at times the stone images of the Madonna and the Child in certain of the *Cantigas* can be seen to assume different positions in separate panels. Now these different positions are not due to the fact that the images are supposed to move, for in the case I am discussing they are no more than parts of the background scene. And yet, in *cantiga* 18, for example, the images do indeed change position. A glance at the page of miniatures will show that the images in the first and second panels at the top of the page are in a different posture from those in the last two panels at the bottom. At the top the Virgin is clasping the Child tightly against her face—a little closer in the second panel at the top than in the first—almost as if she were about to kiss Him. In the last two panels, the Child is sitting placidly in his mother's lap, and his head is not even near that of the Virgin. Still other differences are manifest on the page. In the left bottom panels, the Virgin's right hand is resting upon her knee and her left is on the Child's shoulder. If an artist were sketching as he watched a dramatic presentation of a miracle, he might have caught the actress, who represented the statue, in different positions as she shifted about

The Cantigas de Santa María

in order to rest. I have no proof of any of this, of course, but it seems a fairly good explanation of the images' altered positions.

Realism—almost photographic realism—is an outstanding characteristic of Alfonsine miniatures. Life in these illustrations is depicted in all of its shades and colors, in its beautiful and uplifting aspects, as well as in its base and ugly ones. One sees angels with pastel-shaded wings ministering to mortals (*cantiga* 7), and driving away devils (3); the Virgin banishes demons and resuscitates a monk (11); a beautiful landscape, one of scores to be found, can be seen in 121. But ugliness in appearance, as well as in action, often comes to the eye—even the gross and the scurrilous: *cantiga* 17 may be the worst, for in it is depicted a young man having sexual intercourse with his own mother, while later she disposes of their offspring by dropping it into an open latrine; in number 38 there appears a group of young rascals carousing, drinking, and throwing dice; in another (124) a man is first stoned, then speared and finally slashed across the throat from which his life's blood gushes; a naked penitent is revealed kneeling before the font, while the priest pours baptismal water over him. His genitalia and the darkness of his pubic hair are perfectly visible (46).

In this realism, of course, there was no attempt at the pornographic: it was simply a depiction of life as people were used to seeing it. Naked penitents did kneel in churches; men did have their throats cut; perhaps pregnant women were stabbed in the abdomen and their children removed right in the street by a form of Caesarian section (284). The *Cantigas*, a book of miracles, but all the same a book of secular and not ecclesiastical production and conception, portrayed what there was to portray, and little apparently was concealed or disguised.

Astonishingly minor details appear in these pictures. A scene laid in a forest will contain varieties of fauna and flora. Violets, mosses, and tiny wild flowers, as well as shrubs and trees, can be noted, although sometimes it requires a magnifying glass to see them. In 44 a pair of quail hide among tussocks of grass, rabbit hounds pursue and catch their prey, and falcons dive after larks. Realism, and certainly not impressionism, is the forte of the *Cantigas de Santa María*, though the latter is often present.

The artistic composition of the miniatures is handled with consummate skill. Whole scenes and panoramas on land and on sea are laid down as the backdrops for miracles. The groupings of figures is artistic, and their attitudes and poses reveal their emotions and reactions to events (175); hands are thrown up in horror (4); faces are twisted in fear or glow with laughter (38); a man grimaces and turns his head while his foot is amputated (37).

If perspective is lacking, the very absence of it produces pleasing effects. The passengers on a ship, for example, appear far too enlarged for verisimilitude, but this is so that they can be seen in complete detail, and the effect is not at all displeasing (172]. Occasionally, the artists saved themselves work, much as they do today, by concealing the bare feet of individuals behind walls, stones, or grass, so as to avoid the necessity of painting these appendages, always difficult to portray faithfully (22).

The human figure, in the main, is so well depicted that one feels positive that the artists used living models. The movement of limbs, as well as their position beneath garments is graphically displayed and all proportions of the human body are carefully presented. And the nude, though not seen in many of the *cantigas* —for that matter rare in all medieval manuscripts—is well represented. Guerrero Lovillo cites *cantiga* 60 in which are seen the nude Adam and Eve in the Garden, and says that their figures are not well portrayed. He is quite correct, for they are stiff and massive-limbed. But other nudes or near-nudes have the realistic photographic quality already alluded to. In number 22 there is a truly handsome young man, standing before his enemies in *bragas,* "underwear," and a skin-tight undershirt. His arms, neck, and torso are shapely, and his bare thighs and calves display the play and bulge of muscle in his tense stance. Young gamblers appear in number 38 and in 76 with powerfully thewed limbs and well-defined pectoral muscles. In number 46, mentioned above, a naked penitent, middle-aged and bearded, kneels fully revealed even to his genitalia. In 95 one sees a nude man sitting on the edge of a bed in which a nude woman reclines, her lower extremities under the cover. Both are well and realistically portrayed. A demon in the background is so muscular as to be of heroic proportions.

The plastic artistry in the *Cantigas de Santa María* is, then, an important milestone in the history of Spanish painting. One understands Alfonso's preoccupation with the book's final disposition, even in the great confusion and sorrow of his last illness, and why he felt constrained to mention it in his last will and testament. I translate:

Likewise we order that all the books of the *Songs of Praise of Holy Mary* be in that church where our body shall be interred, and that they be sung on the feast days of Holy Mary. And if that one who inherits legally and by our will what is ours, should wish to own these books of the *Songs of Holy Mary,* we order that he therefore make good compensation to the church from whence he removes them so that he may have grace without sin.[31]

The *Cantigas*—at least manuscript T.j.I—remained in the Cathedral of Seville, where the King's body was interred. Philip II had the collection removed to his library in the Escorial where it is displayed today in a glass case together with Alfonso's astrolabe and other of his possessions.

CHAPTER 6

The Cantigas Profanas *of Alfonso X*

ALFONSO X, as was mentioned in Chapter 3, did not confine his poetic composition to the sacred songs of the *Cantigas de Santa María,* discussed in the previous chapter. His versatility led him into other fields of poetic endeavor, and although his extant *cantigas profanas,* "profane canticles," are relatively few in number, scarcely more than thirty in all, these far from sacred poems represent an important part of his literary career. Some were written when he was a young man, even before he became king, it is thought; but others seem to have been written during his reign and must have appeared even during the years in which he produced the *Cantigas de Santa María* and some of the scientific and legalistic works.

These *cantigas profanas* belong, as did most lyric verse in those times, to the Galician-Portuguese school of versification, and illustrate the fact that the King could compose skilfully in both the traditions of that school as well as under the influence of the Provençal school.

I *Galician-Portuguese Poetry*

In order to understand better just what these traditions are, it will be necessary to discuss, but only in brief and general terms, something of the backgrounds of Galician poetry. The subject in its entirety is far too vast to cover in a single chapter, and moreover, there is no need for such lengthy treatment here when so many excellent studies exist in books and articles distributed through the libraries of this country and abroad.[1]

Galician poetry, like all folk poetry in Europe, must be traced back to ancient varieties of verse which were always closely interwoven with melody and dance. Like many European folk songs surviving in rural areas today, all three components—words, music, and dance—were important in that ancient poetry. No one in those times thought of the words of such songs as elements separate from the other two elements, for these old poems were always sung and always accompanied by dancing.

European folk lyrics or dance songs seem to have sprung up among the primitive agricultural societies, even before the days of the Roman Empire, and were associated with rites connected with plowing, seeding the land, harvesting and milling and vintning. When later Phoenician, Greek, and Roman fertility rites reached the area, these mingled with the primitive native customs and became integral elements of these. Apparently no great changes were occasioned. Nor was there great change in the medieval development of these folk songs. They had, it is true, shed a good deal of their primitive and pagan backgrounds, but they were still verses set to melodies for dancing at harvest festivals and other such seasonal occasions. They were still true folk poetry, and though the Galician language had replaced the ancient languages in which the songs had been sung, and though paganism had long been replaced by Christianity, the old basic foundations of primitive folk song survived.

The same history could be given for folk poetry in France or in any European land, for the folk everywhere develop their songs in much the same way and for much the same reasons. Even the erudite troubadour poetry of Provence, which would influence courtly verse in much of Europe, Galicia included, had arisen from the humble folk poetry in southern France.

In Galicia, then, from time immemorial, a lyric folk poetry had existed and had been active in the lives of the peasants, fisherman and hunters of that land so remote from the currents of European culture. What more natural then that professional minstrels should use these native products in the songs they sang to entertain their compatriots? Quite probably foreign innovations did not prove successful among the lower classes, and this may explain partly, at least, why the native poetic tradition was so powerful and why Galician-Portuguese folk lyric became and remained for centuries the national lyric poetry of Spain and Portugal.

The minstrel, known in Spanish as the *juglar* and in Portuguese as the *jogral,* it is true, in an effort at some originality and for the sake of variety in his lyrical presentations, often reworked the native product, that is, the already established and individual songs; but when he did so, the alterations were slight and the native style, meters, vocabulary and subject matter overshadowed all innovation. One can observe, by the way, the same phenomena in the rise of another form of folk poetry, also designed at first for song and dance. This was the Spanish *romance*, "ballad," a genre created by the folk, dear to the folk, and demanded by the folk when the *juglar* performed in village squares or at rural peasant gatherings. The parallels between the origins and functions of ballads in Castilian and folk lyrics in Galician are many, and so close are these elements that one can find poems in each of these distinct genres which are similar in subject matter and function, differing only in metrical form.

Up to this point the folk lyric of Galicia was a part of oral tradition, for even the *juglares* were singers and did not write on paper the songs they borrowed from the folk or composed in folk meters about folk subjects. In the twelfth century, and to a greater extent in the thirteenth, however, European culture and erudition was spreading across the Pyrenees and penetrating the Iberian Peninsula, even reaching the remote mountains of Galicia. Pilgrims passing through Provence, indeed, pilgrims from Provence and *juglares* and troubadours, too, traversed the famous Road of St. James on their way to the shrine of the saint at Compostela. Spanish monarchs in Aragon, Castile, and León (of which last Galicia was a part), welcomed these travelers and often employed Provençal poets and made them a part of their courts. Alfonso himself befriended such men and learned from them the niceties of their troubadour art. As a result of these contacts, and the popularity and vogue of Provençal courtly lyrics in many parts of Europe, a school of erudite Galician and Castilian poets grew up in Spain, who followed the tenets of Provence, who wrote for kings, princes, and nobles, who demanded the artistic skill and sophistication of poets beyond the Pyrenees. Soon Spanish kings, princes, nobleman, and even commoners wrote in the style of Provence and hardly realized that beneath that style lay the ancient framework of the native verse. But we, who look back upon and analyze the work of the Galician poets writing under the spell of Provençal style, find that native poetry did not die. Actually, even the most devoted proponents of the style of Provence merely grafted upon the firm and fixed roots of the old folk poetry innovations in meter, syntax, vocabulary, and subject matter suggested by the poets of southern France.

Apparently it was almost impossible for Galician poets, even royal and noble poets, to escape the influence of the native lyric. Gerald Brenan in his excellent treatment of Galician verse points out the way in which such people imbibed the native tradition from earliest childhood. "Now in Galicia and Portugal," he writes, "there was a custom known as *amadigo* by which the children of the upper classes were farmed out with peasant nurses in the houses of *vilãoes* or villeins, and grew up almost to manhood with them. It would not be surprising, therefore, if in after-life they felt the *sabor* or charm of this peasant life, as Gil Vicente and Lope de Vega did in the sixteenth century, and rewrote the dance poems of the village girls to express their sentiments about it. No doubt they had love affairs with these girls in which their feelings really played a part, whereas in Provence the cult of love for married women led to an entirely different orientation of erotic feelings and consequently of subjects for poetry." [2]

Alfonso himself, it will be recalled, was reared in the country, and quite probably in Galicia, by noble nurses and guardians who might well have allowed him to have close contacts with rural people. Or, perhaps, his tie with the native songs came through association with folk singers and camp minstrels while he was being trained as a soldier. Whatever the link may have been with native poetry, Alfonso never was able to break away from it entirely. He, like many of the erudite troubadours he subsidized, or who wrote independent of his patronage, would always praise the excellence of the Provençal school. They would write derisively, as Alfonso did against the poet Pero da Ponta,[3] because the man did not write as Provençal poets wrote, and would believe that they followed only Provençal styles. But most of these poets, and Alfonso especially, would always compose some of their songs in the native way. Their *cantigas de amigo* and their *mayas* or May-songs would attest to this.

It is quite certain that Galician erudite poetry survived until well into the fifteenth century, whereas the courtly lyric of Provence did not, because the former never lost touch with its folkloristic origins and the latter lost all contact with its own. Gerald

Brenan probably expresses more graphically than any one what happened to the poetry of the troubadours of southern France. "The extreme elaboration of the Provençal lyric, once its dance accompaniment was dropped and the tune subordinated to the words, carried it beyond the range of the feelings and associations that had given birth to it into a cascade of verbal fireworks where it became dessicated." [4]

Galician traditions of versification and subject matter held their own, therefore. Indeed, after Alfonso's time, Galician poets who had so eagerly turned toward Provence for models, veered sharply away from those models and back toward the ancient native traditions. This can be seen clearly in the poems of King Diniz of Portugal and in the songs of the troubadours who frequented his court. In other words, Galician poetry had started with the folk; had later been taken up by professional minstrels or *juglares,* who altered it little; had then been borrowed and adapted by the troubadours who followed the lead of poets in Provence; and had at last drifted away from Provençal forms and back to the familiar poetry of the people. This evolution brought, it is true, something new to the old poetic style. The learned poets of the *cancioneiros* were erudites who wrote in a polished fashion, but they wrote nevertheless after an ancient style and produced a poetry that was fresh and different from other erudite schools.

II The Great "Cancioneiros"

Mentioned in Chapter 3, but not named, were the great anthologies of song called *cancioneiros,* "books of poems," in which were found the two thousand poems by the two hundred named poets. Only the three considered below have survived the ages, but it is quite likely that others were made and later lost. Perhaps the fact that all three contained the contributions of such kings as Alfonso X and Diniz of Portugal caused these anthologies to be preserved. The *Cancioneiro da Ajuda,* so called because it was discovered in the library of Ajuda in Portugal, is the oldest and represents the Galician-Portuguese lyric under the strongest influence from Provence. It is of great interest in that it reveals the extent of the borrowing of metrical forms and because its poets are numbered among the oldest of the Galician troubadours.

The *Canzoniere Portoghese della Biblioteca Vaticana,* whose
Italian title is owed to the fact that it was copied from the lost
Galician original by an Italian, who did not, by the way, tamper
with the text or translate the poems into his language. It was
found in the Vatican Library, and this explains the other part of
the name the manuscript bears. The *Cancioneiro Colocci-Brancuti*
bears the title it has because it belonged to a sixteenth-century
humanist named Angelo Colocci de Cagli, and later to the Mar-
quis of Brancuti. Both the *Vaticana* and the *Colocci-Brancuti* are
anthologies of poets of the thirteenth and fourteenth centuries;
both contain poems written under the full influence of Provençal
style and the later Galician school which had somewhat freed
itself from that foreign style; and both have poems written by
the Learned King. In the *Vaticana* Alfonso is represented by nineteen songs—numbers 61–79—and in the *Colocci-Brancuti* by
twelve—numbers 467–78. Neither of these manuscripts contains
the musical notations one would expect to find in a *cancioneiro*
or song book.[5]

It is no longer doubted that Alfonso composed the poems ascribed to him in the *cancioneiros.* The Alfonso listed as author
of these poems—"El rei Dom Affonso de Castella e de Leom"—
has been proved to be Alfonso X by Cesare de Lollis in a lengthy
article.[6]

III   *Alfonso's "Cantigas de Amigo"*

The Learned King was especially adept at composing the native *cantigas de amigo.* Recall that these were originally the pas-
sionate laments of lovelorn maidens pining for absent lovers or
indifferent sweethearts. Recall, too, that Galician troubadours, all
of whom were men, wrote erudite *cantigas de amigo,* putting
verses into the mouths of imaginary country girls. The selection
which follows, taken from the repertory of the Learned King,
will illustrate quite well just how impassioned, sentimental, romantic, and subjective such poems sounded. It would appear that
Alfonso composed this lyric, basing it upon the old Galician tradition; but it is not impossible that he simply wrote down a
cantiga de amigo which he had learned from the folk, altering
it only very slightly. We cannot prove this to be true, of course,

but one can suspect it of Alfonso in his guise of troubadour-poet. He certainly collected, or caused to be collected, various of the miracles of the Virgin from popular, folkloristic sources and included these in the *Cantigas de Santa María:* Might he not as well have collected folk lyrics for the erudite anthologies being put together in his times?

Translation cannot ever convey the true and exact flavor and feeling of a *cantiga de amigo* like the one to follow. Nor can Engglish, since it has no generic agreement of adjectives with their nouns, reveal that a woman is supposed to be the singer of the song. But a glance at the Galician-Portuguese below will reveal that the last word of the first line, *coitada,* is feminine, indicating that *eu coitada,* "wretched me," is indeed a damsel.

These poems contain a good deal of *double-entendre,* their vocabularies are archaic and even the very syntax and grammar are unorthodox and at times inexplicable.

Oh, wretched me!	(*Ay! eu coitada*
how I live	*como viuo*
In great sorrow	*En gram cuydado*
for my lover	*por meu amigo*
who has gone away!	*Que ey alongado!*
Long does my lover	*Muyto me tarda*
delay me	*o meu amigo*
in the waiting.	*na guarda!*
Oh, wretched me!	*Ay! eu coitada*
how I live	*como viuo*
In great desire	*Em gram deseio*
for my lover	*por meu amigo*
who delays and whom I don't see!	*Que tarda e non ueio!*
Long does my lover	*muyto me tarda*
delay me	*O meu amigo*
in the waiting!	*na guarda!*)

IV *Alfonso's "Cantigas de Escarnio"*

Many, in fact the majority of the King's *cantigas profanas* are best classified as *cantigas de escarnio,* "songs of mockery." An excellent contemporary description of these songs appears in the anthology *Colocci-Brancuti,* which I have translated as follows:

Songs of mockery are those which the troubadours write, wishing to speak evil of someone in them, and they say it in enigmatic words, which have two meanings for those who do not understand; and these words are called equivocations by learned men. . . .

They were, then, songs of mordant criticism, and by allusion and implication they mock those at whom they are directed. In most cases the poets of the court of Alfonso must have known perfectly well who the victims were. The king directed such metrical attacks upon several categories of people—loose women, reprobate clergymen, cowardly knights, poets he considered un-skilled, and fops, to name the most important. His words are harsh, to the point, and sometimes cruel. Number 75 of the *Vati-can* codex is a scathing criticism of men who overdress.

Vaticana 75

Now I would gladly like to know
about these who wear skirts with sashes,
in which they squeeze themselves very often,
whether they do it to show their loins
so that their ladies whom they have not pleased
may be pleased with them.
     Oh God, if some one would only tell me
why they wear these very wide silken sashes,
like pregnant women,
whether it is thereby to gain good
from those with whom they never know how to speak,
except in the country, or whether they are well made.
     I do not see them cause it [their loins] to be hidden
with the upturned ends of their mantles,
which resembles the snare of the bird-traps,
when the flies come to afflict them
thence whether they intend to deceive them thereby
in order that they may be enamored of them.
     Likewise I also see them wear
very short and puffed sleeves,
just as if they were manuring fields
or if they wished to knead tarts,
or perhaps they do it to fodder
their horses if they were fed with barley.

(De gradó queria ore gaber
d'estes que traem sayas encordadas,
em que s'apertam muy prontas vegadas
se o fazem pol os ventres mostrar;
porque se devam d'eles a pagar
sas senhores que nom tem pagadas.

Ay deus, se me quizess'alguem dizer
porque tragem estas cintas sirgadas
muyt'anchas, como mulheres prenhadas,
s'e em eles per hi gaanhar
bem das com que nunca sabem falar
ergo nas terras se som bem lauradas.

Encobrir nom o lhes vejo fazer
com as pontas dos mantos trastornadas
em que semelha as aboys das aferradas
quando as moscas les veem coitar
d'en se as cuidan per hi d'enganar
que sejam d'eles por en namoradas.

Outrosy lhis ar vejo trager
mangas mui curtas et enfunadas,
bem como se adubassem quartadas
ou se quizessem tortas amassar,
ou quiçá o fazem por deliurar
sas bestas se fossem acevadadas.)

An excellent example of his attacks upon the fair-weather soldier who preferred the joys of home to the rigors of war with the
Moor is number 69 of the Vatican text. I have translated only the
first stanza:

Vaticana 69
Dom João, when he arrived here this year
first and saw the turn of the war,
had such a great desire to go home
that he immediately took his heart as his leader,
in order to get away from the war the sooner,
and it caused him to leave there
reputation and bravery, and he went over the hill.

(Dom João, quand'ogano aqui chegou
primeiramente e vyu vôlta a guerra
tam gram sabor ouve d'ir a sa terra

[104]

que logu'então por adail filhou
seu coraçom; e el fex-lh'y leyxar
polo mais toste da guerr'alongar
prez e esforço, e passou a serra.)

V   *Alfonso's "Cantigas de mal dizir"*

The King composed *cantigas de maldizir,* "songs of malediction," against various people and institutions. Such songs are best explained in the Introduction to the Colocci-Brancuti text, from which I translate a passage:

Songs of malediction are those which the troubadours make more openly; in them appear words which intend to speak evil and do not have any other meaning than that which they state clearly. . . .

In these songs there is no implication or allusion, but a direct and open attack in which the person is named to his shame. One of the most mordant and lewd is that leveled against Maria Peres, who was known as "a Balteyra," a poem that reveals Alfonso as a poet not always pious or devout, as was the case in the well-known *Cantigas de Santa María,* or in the innocent *cantigas de amigo.* Maria Peres, by the way, was a famous *soldadera,* "half-prostitute, half-entertainer and camp follower." Her companion in sin was Mayor Cotum, also mentioned in the poem. The tone of the *cantiga* is unmistakable, and the matter of going "to take the measure" of the Balteyra can only mean one obscene thing and hardly needs to be explained. The same is true of Joham Rodriguiz' "shaft."

Vaticana 64

Joham Rodriguiz went to take Balteyra's
measure, so that she could accommodate his shaft,
and he said: if you wish to succeed, you
must receive it of just this length
and not in any other way.
    And he said: this is the entire shaft,
and it is not only to you that I give the whole thing,
and since it must be received with no stint,
it should be that full length
in order to attain the yardstick's full measure.

. . . .

 And he said: this is the Spanish measure,
not the measure of Lombardy or of Germany,
and because it is large, let it not trouble you,
because a slender one is worth nothing for a large thing,
and I know that Anna is much more sufficient for this.

 (Joham Rodriguiz for desinar a Belteyra
ssa medida, perque colha a medeyra
e disse: se bem queredes fazer,
de tal midida a devedes acolher
e nom meor per nulha maneyra.
 E disse: esta é a madeyra inteyra
e de mais nom na dey eu a vós sinlheyra,
e pois que sem compasso a de meter
a tan longa deve toda seer
pera as traspernas da scaleyra.

. . . .

 E disse: esta é a medida de Espanha
cá nom de Lombardia nem d'Alamanha,
e porque é grossa nom vos seja mal,
cá delgada pera tanta rem nom val
e d'esto muy mays sey eu c'abond'Anha.)

Vicious, scurrilous and obscene is the King's attack upon the Dean of Calez. Apparently that worthy was addicted to a very sensual life and had perfected himself in the art of sexual pleasure through books written on the subject. One envisages his library, the shelves filled with copies of Ovid's *Amores* and perhaps various oriental tomes like the Arabic translation of the *Kama Sutra* or of Sheik Umar ibn Muhammed al-Nefzawi's *The Perfumed Garden*. Apparently Alfonso had either heard of the Dean's amorous activities or had perhaps observed some of the ecclesiastic's comings and goings on amorous missions. At any rate he composed a *cantiga de maldizir* that is rough, to the point, and most illustrative of this particular variety of Galician-Portuguese poetry. In translating such a piece it is always difficult to know how to render the word *foder*, whose English equivalents are all generally regarded as unprintable. I have rendered it by the word "futter," not found in English dictionaries, but employed—perhaps invented by Sir Richard Burton—in his renowned transla-

tion *The Thousand Nights and a Night* from the Arabic. This
seems a better choice to me than such expressions as "to have
intercourse with," or "to copulate with."

Vaticana 76
I found books that were being
carried to the Dean of Calez to read,
and I asked the one who was taking them
about them, and he replied to me: Sir
with these books that you see as gifts,
and with the others which he has of his own,
he is able to futter as much as he desires.

For I will tell you even more about this,
indeed, all I know of his deeds,
for by my faith, he, through the books
that he has, I know not the woman
whom he has not caused to see ravens
as cranes or eagles as snails,
so as to futter her if he wished.

For there is nothing more in the art of intercourse
than is found in the books that he owns,
and he has such great joy in reading them
that never, by night or day, does he do anything else;
and he knows so well about the art of futtering,
that with his books that he has about this art
he futters Moorish women whenever he pleases.

And with all this he still does more,
using the books that he has, upon my word;
and if he finds a woman who is suffering
from that disease known as Saint Martial's fire,
he so bewitches her through futtering,
that while he is at this act with her,
he makes her fever seem nothing more than snow or frost.

(*Ao dayão de Calez eu achey*
liuros que lhi levavam da leger,
e ó que os tragia preguntey
por elles, e respondeu-m'el: senhor
como estes liuros que vós veedes, dons
e com os outros que ele tem dos sons
ffod'er por eles quanto foder quer.
Ca inda vos end'eu mais direy
cá tam mal e muyt'a fee leer

por quant'en sa fazenda sey
com os liuros que tem, nom a mulher
a que nom faça que semelhe grous
os corvos et as aguias babous
per força de foder se x'el quiser.

> *Cá nom ha mais na arte do foder,*
> *do que nos liuros que el tem, jaz,*
> *e el ha tal sabor de os leer*
> *que nunca noite nem dia al faz,*
> *e sabe d'arte de foder tam bem*
> *que c'os seus liuros d'artes que el tem*
> *fod'el as mouras cada que lhi praz.*

> *E com tod'est aynda faz al*
> *com os liuros que tem, per boa fé,*
> *se acha molher que aja mal*
> *d'este fogo que de Sam Marçal é,*
> *assy vae per foder encantar*
> *que fohendo lhi faz bem semelhar*
> *que é geada, ou neve, nom al.)*

VI *Other Varieties of Cantigas*

And yet, despite the ability of the King to sink to such attacks upon deans, camp followers, and other people he disliked or scorned, he could compose a beautiful *maya*, "May-song," like this one which Martín de Riquer valued highly enough to include in his *Historia de la Literatura Universal.*[7] I translate it here *in toto*:

> Well may you come, May, and with joy.
> Wherefore let us beg Saint Mary
> that she may ever beseech her Son
> to protect us from error and folly.
> Well may you come, May, and with joy.

> Well may you come, May, and with health.
> Wherefore let us praise her of great virtue
> that she may beg God to aid us always
> against the devil and to shield us from him.
> Well may you come, May, and with joy,

> (*Ben vennas, mayo, et con alegria.*
> *Poren roguemos a Santa Maria*

que a seu Fillo rogue todavia
que el nos guarde d'err'e folia.
Ben vennas, mayo, et con alegria.

Ben vennas, mayo, con toda saude.
Porque loemos a de gran vertude
que a Deus rogue que nos sempr'ajude
contra o dem'e de si nos escude.
Ben vennas, mayo, et con alegria.)

And one of his *cantigas* in the *Cancioneiro Colucci-Brancuti,*
number 409, is nothing less than a *cantiga de loor* addressed to
the Blessed Virgin. Indeed it appears as *cantiga* 40 of the *Cantigas de Santa María,*[8] and must have been a favorite hymn of
Alfonso. I shall offer the translation of only its first two parts:

Colocci-Brancuti 409
God keep you glorious
Queen Mary,
Light of the saints, beautiful,
and roadway to heaven.
[God] keep you, who conceived,
Very much contrary to nature,
since you have given birth to your **Father**
and remained pure
Virgin, and therefore you ascended
above the heights
of heaven because you desired
That which He wished . . .
God keep you glorious
Queen Mary,
Light of the saints, beautiful,
and roadway to heaven.

(*Deus te salue gloriosa*
reinha Maria,
Lume dos sanctos, fremosa
e dos ceos uij[a].
Salue te, que concebiste
Mui contra natura
E pois tue Padre pariste
E ficasti pura
Virgen e por en sobiste

Sobre la altura
Dos ceos porque quisisti
O que El queria
Deus te salue gloriosa
reinha Maria,
Lume dos sanctos, fremosa
e dos ceos uija.)

One last poem, rare because it is written not in Galician-Portuguese, but in the King's own native tongue, Castilian, will end
the selections of his poetry presented in this chapter. This is a
short prayerful poem which may be the only lyric piece Alfonso
composed in Spanish.

Lady, for the love of God
have some pity for me,
for my eyes like rivers
run from the day that I saw thee;
Brothers and cousins and uncles,
all have I lost for you,
If thou dost not think of me
Here.

(*Senhora, por amor de Dios*
aved alguno duelo de my,
que los mis ojos como rrios
corren del dia que uos uy;
Ermanos e primos e tyos,
todo-los yo por uos perdy.
Se uos non pensades de my
Fy.)[9]

King Alfonso, then as he is represented in the selections assigned to him in the great *cancioneiros*, appears as a versatile poet
of the Galician-Portuguese school. Deeply influenced by the lyric
style of the elegant Provençal troubadours, and convinced that
he followed this style, he, like many poets in his time, nonetheless composed also in the native Galician tradition. His *cantigas
profanas*, whether couched in the meters of Provence, or in the
simple form of the Galician folk, form an important part of his
poetic creativity and should not be overlooked when one studies
his poetic genius.

CHAPTER 7

The Legal Treatises

I Law in Spain Before Alfonso

SPACE does not permit a lengthy discussion of the legal treatises of Alfonso X. The importance of these great works, nevertheless, their magnitude, their effect upon contemporary and subsequent laws, both in the homeland and the colonies, demands some treatment. Indeed, the *Siete Partidas*,[1] "The Seven Divisions of Law," Alfonso's most voluminous legal codex, even touched upon certain forms of medieval literature which will be stressed and developed later in this chapter. First, however, I must present some statement of these legal treatises in the development of Spanish law.

When Alfonso was crowned, the state of Spanish law was, to him at least, deplorable. He discusses this in one of the versions of the *Siete Partidas*, and what he says is worth reading in translation: ". . . and we, the above-mentioned King Don Alfonso, understanding and seeing the great evils which were born and which arose among the people of our realm due to the many *fueros*, 'custom laws' practiced in the towns and in the country, which are against God and against justice; and realizing that some people were judged outrageously and without reason and others by laws lacking legality; and that they even erased[2] and wrote what seemed to their own advantage and to the harm of the common people, taking away from the Kings their power and their rights and doing that which ought not to be done at all. And for all these causes justice and law were lacking, for those who had to judge cases could not render their judgments with certainty and completeness; rather, they judged at hazard and according to personal whim, and those who received harm could not obtain justice or redress as they deserved. Wherefore, we, in order to remove all of these evils which we have set down, made these laws, which are written in this book for the service of God and for the common good of all people in our domains. And may they learn to strive to keep themselves from error so that they will not suffer punishment." [3]

The King, then, had ample reason to examine the law of the land and to find it wanting. Student of jurisprudence that he was, he knew the legal history of early Spain. The Visigoths, when they had conquered Roman Spain in the fifth century, had brought with them a body of law founded upon two ancient heritages—Germanic custom law, unwritten for generations, and certain Roman codices which they had debased and molded to their own needs. This ancient *Lex Gothica,* as it was called, had, by the seventh century, been set down in Latin with the title *Forum Judicum,* "Laws of the Judges." It would continue to be the law in Asturias, and later in León, and to a lesser extent in Castile, until well into the fourteenth century. By Alfonso's time, however, the *Forum Judicum* had been translated into Spanish at the behest of his father, Ferdinand, with the title *Fuero Juzgo.*

Castile, a frontier county until it freed itself from León in 1035 and became a kingdom, had not always been able to follow the tenets of the *Fuero Juzgo.* Remote in many of its areas, in others bordering upon the hostile territory of the Moor, it lay beyond the reach of legal experts and even of legal documents. The need to make laws that would serve the new situations arising from frontier life led to *fueros* based upon the customs of the region, upon precedent, and even upon the memory of what had been law in more settled and civilized areas. As the towns grew in Castile, the burghers collected such custom law and set it down in books of their own making, and these substituted for the older codes. Later, as the towns grew and developed civic organization, their inhabitants asked the king and the nobles in whose lands their towns were situated to ratify their *fueros* and to give them charters. King and nobleman alike generally complied, for the towns, as was pointed out in Chapter 1, were powerful allies to their rulers and important in the development of far-flung possessions. With the charters which the towns secured came the beginnings of independence, and eventually even a voice in the early *cortes,* or parliaments. Their importance, therefore, continued to grow and without them the history of Spain would have taken a different course in those perilous times. "The cities and towns of

Castile and León, however," wrote Dr. Evelyn Proctor, "unlike those of northern France, but like some of the cities of southern France and the Italian communes, exercised jurisdiction over wide territories outside the city walls including villages, smaller towns, and the lands of knights and lesser nobles. . . . Thus a network of laws of local application was spread over the kingdom." [4]

II *Alfonso's Lesser Legal Codes*

Nevertheless, in spite of the fact that charters existed, *fueros* of regional variety continued to be the law in more remote parts of the kingdom. To an erudite like Alfonso, and to the legal experts in Roman Law employed by him, the situation must have seemed almost completely chaotic. Immediately, then, after the death of Ferdinand in 1252 and Alfonso's subsequent coronation in the same year, the new King began to improve the legal code of the realm. It was not entirely his own idea, of course, for King Ferdinand had seen the need and had instilled in his son both an interest in the law and the desire to improve it. Indeed, King Ferdinand may have actually carried one code of laws, the *Setenario*, through its final redaction, although some authorities believe that it was his son who brought it to conclusion. Whether the contribution of Ferdinand or of Alfonso, it was the first of the four legal codices written in the thirteenth century and may be regarded as the first draft of the *Siete Partidas*, or at least the first draft of *Partida* I. The object of this code was to make a selection of the best laws found in the many *fueros* and charters—including, of course, the *Fuero Juzgo*—to encompass both general and municipal documents, and to create a single body of law that would be general throughout the domain, superseding all previous codes, thereby bringing about uniformity and the elimination of abuses and the evils resulting therefrom.

The *Setenario* did not accomplish all that King Ferdinand, and later Alfonso, had envisaged. The latter, however, may not have been nearly so idealistic as his father in the matter, for he realized that it was not feasible in a single lifetime to alter existing law by simply creating a new legal code, for old laws yield slowly to change and replacement. It is more likely that Alfonso hoped to systematize existing law and to unify it by degrees, step by step, allowing changes to develop gradually.

Another legal code, known as the *Fuero Real,* "Royal Fuero," the only body of law actually to be promulgated by Alfonso, seems to have been completed early in Alfonso's reign, probably before 1255, a year in which it was granted to some ten cities and towns. Sahagún, Valladolid, Palencia, Peñafiel, Soria, Cuéllar, Burgos, Buitrago, Avila, and Alarcón all received it, as did later Escalona and the towns of Extremadura. This shows, however, that it did not apply to all of Castile and León. Furthermore, it did not supersede existing laws, charters, and *fueros* and was valid only in so far as it did not run counter to these. Judges, however, used it in cases of appeal in the king's court, and thus it had dignity and force. The book is concise and clear in its presentation of law, but is by no means as complete and detailed as the later *Siete Partidas.* Still, as law, pure and simple, it must have been much more practical in the hands of lawyers and judges than the longer work. Matters like the appointment of mayors and other civil officials, procedures in lawsuits held in municipal courts, and laws regulating marriage, sales, inheritance, and debt all are to be found in it methodically treated and presented. The *Fuero Real* drew somewhat from the old *Fuero Juzgo,* but not as substantially as had been supposed until recently; it was based for the most part on the *Fuero de Soria* from which Galo Sánchez, who edited this latter *fuero,* reveals that some one-fifth of its provisions were taken; and it must have borrowed from other *fueros,* although no complete analysis has been made of all its sources. It served, too, in its own turn, as a source of later law books and especially of the Learned King's *Siete Partidas.* Perhaps its greatest contribution was the unifying force it exerted upon the chaos of existing laws, charters, and *fueros.* Though it was never popular or decisive in the face of the towns' jealously cherished *fueros,* it was a valuable beginning of new laws because it made some attempt to curtail the powers of the nobles who lived within the jurisdiction of some of the towns.

The third of the lesser legalistic treatises of Alfonso is the *Espéculo de las Leyes,* "Mirror of the Laws," and though it was the last codex that he actually sponsored, following even the long and comprehensive *Siete Partidas,* it will be discussed here only very briefly, leaving the balance of the chapter to the treatment of the most important and longest of the king's laws. Evelyn Proctor discusses some of the problems posed by any study of the *Espéculo*. "At what date was it written? Was it ever promulgated? What is its relationship to the *Siete Partidas?* These questions are clearly interrelated. It has been variously described as a brief compilation which, together with the *Fuero Real*, was intended to fill the gap until a complete code could be compiled, and also a rough draft of the *Partidas*, either of which interpretations entails a date of composition earlier than 1256, or alternatively, as a later compilation reflecting the views of the supporters of Sancho IV. The prologue categorically states that the book was intended to be used in cases of appeal to the king's court, that it was compiled with the advice and consent of the prelates and nobles, of men learned in the law and others of the court, and that a copy of it *seelado con nuestro seello de plomo* (impressed with seal of our lead seal) was sent to every town." [5] In some of its passages it is almost identical with the same passages in the *Partidas*, but in other cases the resemblance is only slight. Apparently, it borrowed from the *Partidas*, and is believed to date from after 1276, whereas the *Partidas* were written between 1256 and 1265.

There are five books in the *Espéculo*. Book I treats of law, the doctrine of the Trinity, and the articles of the Catholic Faith, and if compared with the first *Partida*, will appear as a close parallel; Books II and III deal with military organizations and political groups in the kingdom, matters also found in the second *Partida;* and Books IV and V handle the matter of justice in much the same way as this is treated in the third *Partida*. Of the sixth and seventh books, mentioned in the text of the *Espéculo*, no trace has been found, and it is possible that no such books ever formed a part of the code.

The three shorter books of Alfonsine law—the *Setenario*, the *Fuero Real*, and the *Espéculo de las Leyes*, then, all form important elements in the king's legalistic planning and all served either as preludes, stopgaps or abbreviations of the great *Siete Partidas* to be discussed below.

III Las Siete Partidas

1. *The Value of the* Partidas

From early times Spaniards recognized the merit and excellence of the *Siete Partidas* and were generous in their praise of it. But so were foreign legists; indeed, they have extolled its praises beyond those of any other legal codex. One, Samuel Astley Dunham, who was a friend, by the way, of the English poet Robert Southey, wrote glowingly of it, and his remarks can be taken seriously. Dunham knew Spain well, and his history of Spain and Portugal is still considered an authoritative work. He said of the *Partidas:* "It is by far the most valuable monument of legislation, not merely of Spain, but of Europe, since the publication of the Roman Code. . . . No code in use in the middle ages is to be compared with it for extent, for natural arrangement, for the spirit of justice generally pervading its provisions, or for knowledge. It is, in fact, a complete body of morality and religion, defining the duties of every citizen, from the highest to the lowest station; assigning the grounds for their duties, and deducing one obligation from another with great precision and with some force of reasoning." [6]

The French *Dictionnaire Historique* states: "We find in every page of that work the highest wisdom, and the sternest justice. It gave to the monarch under whose auspices it was executed, titles more appropriate to the epithet of learned bestowed upon him by his contemporaries, than his astronomical researches, and physical scientific knowledge, however surprising the one and the other may have been considered in an age when all studies were so much disregarded. It is in the precious code, that we must seek the early treasures of the Spanish language; there we shall find the characteristic features of that idiom, at a time when it retained yet a simplicity of turn, and form of expression, which gave it more freedom and ease than it now possesses, though written in an age when the language, yet unpolished, preserved much of its primitive rudeness. We, however, perceive in the style of the work a grace, a facility worthy of the elevated sentiments that pervade it; and, in spite of some defects, we believe that the Spanish language, such as it was, when the *Partidas* were compiled, had already arrived at a degree of perfection which the Italian writers did not attain until many years after." [7]

Though some complain that the *Partidas* are not original, such criticism can be overlooked, for originality was not its purpose. The value of the *Siete Partidas* is that it gathered together the then known legalistic wisdom of the ages, especially the knowledge handed down from Rome's legists, and made it available in a vernacular tongue that could be read by those who knew no Latin. Furthermore, once in that vernacular, the *Partidas* not only were able to recast and remold Spanish law, but to disseminate it across such widely dispersed portions of the earth as Western Europe, Africa, Asia, and both North and South America.

2. *Alfonso and His Legists*

This great legal code was first known by the name of *Libro* (or *Fuero*) *de las Leyes* and was not known as the *Siete Partidas* until the following century. No one is certain who the compilers were, but it is known that they produced the great code in seven years, finishing it either in 1263 or 1265. Several names of possible editors have been suggested—an Italian jurist named Azo, a certain Jacobo Ruiz, Fernando Martínez, who became bishop elect of Oviedo in 1269, and Roldán who edited the *Ordenamiento de las Tahurerías,* a title difficult to translate but which meant "Control of the state-owned gambling houses." The great historian Altamira states: "We do not know who were the authors of the *Partidas;* and in view of our ignorance it is not strange that critics ascribe that work to the well-known jurisconsultants of the time, some of whom are cited in this text. . . . The redaction of the *Partidas* was the work of several jurists whose names are not cited in the text, was done under the supervision of Alfonso, who was himself an author of zeal, and was subject (how much cannot be determined) to his active intervention." [8]

Some even ascribe the entire work to the King himself because of its uniformity of plan, the striking similarity of style to that in his other works, an acrostic of his name found in the book, and a clause in his last will and testament executed in Seville in 1283 which states that the *Siete Partidas* is a "book that we have made." That he wrote the entire corpus of these laws is doubtful. The similarity of style and diction can probably be ascribed to the fact that Alfonso actually read, corrected, emended, in short, completely edited every work he sponsored. He actually states this in several places, and I think that we can accept the statement as reliable and true. For example, in the Preface to the *Libro de las Estrellas Fijas*, "Book of the Fixed Stars," he said, and I translate: "And afterwards the aforementioned king (he had spoken of himself earlier in the third person) corrected it and ordered it written, and he struck out the words which he understood to be superfluous and of doubtful meaning and which were not in pure Castilian, and substituted others which he viewed as satisfactory and he himself set the entire writing in order." [9]

Evelyn Proctor points out that Alfonso even chose the sources for certain of the books, if not all of them, and supports her statement with a quote from the Prologue of the *General Historia*, Alfonso's great chronicle of the world: "Wherefore for all these reasons I, Don Alfonso, . . . after I had caused to be assembled many writings and many histories of the deeds of the ancients, I selected from them the most reliable and the best that I knew; and I made therefrom this book and I commanded to be written in it all the well-known deeds and also stories from the Bible, as well as from other great events which had taken place in the world, since the beginning until our own time." [10] There can be little doubt that King Alfonso was the over-all editor-in-chief of the books he sponsored. His personal touch is present in all of them, even to some extent in the translations, although quite naturally in translations he must have had to accept what experts wrote more than in other cases.

3. *The Function of* Las Siete Partidas

Whether Alfonso in his wisdom envisaged any immediate pro-mulgation of the *Siete Partidas,* or desired that it would become the law of the land during his lifetime is open to question. He seemed, rather, to have taken the longer view, hoping that the great codex would be accepted throughout the realm as a kind of legal encyclopedia which judges and lawyers could consult as a guide prepared by noted experts in jurisprudence, including the king himself, in spite of the fact that Alfonso stated in the Prologue that "We are pleased to command that all of our do-minion be governed by these laws and no other." [11] Certainly the political situation, when the nobility was making every effort to retain and even increase its own power to the detriment of royal authority, was not conducive to the strictures found in the *Partidas*. Besides, viewed from practical legalistic aspects, these *Seven Divisions of Law* contained elements of theory and didacticism not relevent to the actual law at all. It seems likely, therefore, that his commands as to the acceptance of the *Partidas* were meant to govern future generations, and that for his own times these laws might best serve as a form of legal education and a preparation for the making of later legal codices. He was aware of the facts as they faced him. The hidalgos had much to lose by the acceptance of the *Partidas* for, since these laws were based upon Roman law and decretals for the most part, they were at variance with the already established custom laws and prejudices, and were opposed openly by nobles whose vested interests were threatened. Altamira goes so far as to say that had the *Partidas* been enforced or enforceable, some considerable chaos might have been the result: ". . . if the immediate imposition of so considerable a mass of innovations upon the cities of the Castilian crown had been possible, the derangements produced in civil life would have been enormous. Fortunately, impositions of this sort are not reconcilable with the processes of history. When attempted they are futile." [12] Alfonso, therefore, did not try to have the *Partidas* promulgated in his lifetime, but he must surely have intended that they become a real body of law for future generations.

Even so, and in spite of sage and conservative beliefs of the King as to the place of the *Partidas* in contemporary life, these laws gained strength. It was at first in the universities that they made their influence felt. In classes where students studied Roman law, the *Partidas* became reference books and texts to be studied. Glosses and notes taken in the margins of the copies of the *Partidas*, penned in the thirteenth and fourteenth centuries, show this, as does the fact that the *Partidas* were read and expounded in Portuguese and Catalonian universities also. Some isolated fragments were even published as doctrinal texts. Moreover, as many great lawyers were at the same time university professors, or had had university training in classes in which the *Partidas* were assigned texts, they were naturally inclined to regard these Alfonsine texts as authoritative in legal theory, as well as actual practice, in courts where judges who knew and had studied them presided. Altamira goes so far as to tell us that "One cannot otherwise understand why, in a number of Cortes (for example those of Segovia in 1347), representations were made to the king against certain details of the *Partidas,* which if they had *not* been enforced, could not fittingly have been characterized by the petitioners as infractions of the law." [13]

Hence the universities of Spain, particularly that of Salamanca, became the great agencies which diffused Roman law and the *Partidas,* based upon Roman law, throughout the Peninsula. Alfonso's great-grandson, Alfonso XI, went so far as to confirm an order by which the *Partidas* were given force in the land, subject to the municipal *fueros,* the *Fuero Real,* and the privileges of the nobles. Thus, more than eighty years after the completion of the *Partidas* they were promulgated as the law of the land toward the end of the reign of Alfonso XI (1310–50). The *Partidas* were printed first in 1491, edited by Alfonso Díaz de Montalvo. Reedited again and again, his text was at last superseded by an edition prepared by the famous legist Gregorio López in 1555. But it was only as late as 1505 that the *Partidas* acquired full force in the *Leyes de Toro,* "Laws of Toro," so named because these *Leyes* were promulgated in that venerable Spanish city.

4. *The Sources of the* Partidas:

a. *Native Sources*

No one has made a detailed study of all the sources of the *Siete Partidas,* possibly because many of its sections stem from old custom law distributed through the *fueros,* some of which have not survived in manuscripts until the present time. There is no doubt, of course, as to the influence of the *Fuero Juzgo,* for documented proof reveals that that great body of law was incorporated into the *Partidas.* The same may be said of the *Fuero Real,* and especially of the *Setenario* which, as has been stated earlier, can be considered as the first draft of the *Partidas* and, according to Scott, even some of the old *Lex Gothica* survives in the Alfonsine codex, notably in number 12 in which inquisition and the presumption of guilt are treated.

b. *Ecclesiastical Sources*

Canon law and other legal tracts of ecclesiastical origin helped also to shape the *Partidas*. PARTIDA I, LAW IN GENERAL; CANON LAW, in most of its pages, stems straight from canon law as found in the Decretals which were issued at various times by the Church and disseminated throughout Christendom. The first formal compilation of canon law of any great importance was the *Decretum* of Gratian which had appeared in Spain as well as in the rest of Europe before the completion of the Alfonsine work. Also the *Decretals* of Gregory IX had been extracted from the *Corpus Juris Canonici*, "Corpus of Canon Law," and compiled by a Spaniard named Raymundo de Peñafort, and this compilation was available to Alfonso and his jurisconsultants.

The importance of ecclesiastical law in all civil codices is stressed by Altamira: "The Renaissance which was brought about in the Church from the time of Gregory VII (1073–85) carried with it an extension of the Church's power, a favorable modification of its relations with the State, and the enlargement of the personal and real immunities of the clergy, the latter being reflected in the practices of civil law. At the same time . . . the Church was . . . subjecting to its jurisdiction and to the rule of the canon law many institutions of the civil law, such as marriage, usurious loans, rent charges, etc. The slow penetration of that law into the customs and statute-books of Castile is particularly observable in the field of family law, beginning with marriage itself, and in certain classes of contract,—not to mention the modifications it produced in the fields of public, political, and criminal law, concession to the crown by the Pope, absolution of the subjects from oath of allegiance, change in criminal procedure." [14]

And of less import, but yet worthy of consideration, were the writings of Gregory the Great, St. Augustine, and St. Bernard, whose moral precepts add a tone of pious doctrinal authority to some of the titles in the *Partidas*.

c. *International Law—Maritime*

Maritime law had by the thirteenth century become international and was set up in two famous codices, the *Rôles d'Ôleron*, "The Lists [of laws] of Ôleron," which dealt with maritime law on the Atlantic, and the *Consulat de la Mer,* "The Regulation of the Sea," on the Mediterranean. Since Spain had coastlines on both seas, the two corpora of maritime law affected her, and both were used in the *Partidas.* Those parts of PARTIDA V which deal with maritime law are so similar to the *Rôles of Ôleron,* which was also the basis of English maritime law, that they appears to have come directly from it.

d. *Roman Law*

Vast and of the greatest importance of all in the *Partidas* was Roman law, notably from the *Code of Justinian* and from the glosses and commentaries of his code written by Italian legists. Indeed, the *Partidas* attempt to unify existing law by basing it upon Roman law, and the universities of Spain collaborated in this in that they taught Roman law almost to the complete exclusion of the laws in the *fueros.* Most of PARTIDA III, PROCEDURE AND PROPERTY, is taken almost exclusively from Roman law, and PARTIDA V, OBLIGATIONS AND MARITIME LAW, is almost word by word from Roman law.

5. *Literary Sources*

In PARTIDA II, PUBLIC LAW; GOVERNMENT AND ADMINISTRATION, such didactic literary works as the *Disciplina Clericalis,* "Scholar's Guide," of the Aragonese Jewish convert, Pedro Alfonso, and the collections of proverbs known as *Bocados de Oro* and the *Poridad de Poridades,* mentioned in Chapter 3, also helped to color the *Partidas.* Possibly a more careful examination than any made to date would reveal other sources of a literary nature.

6. *Dissemination of the* Partidas

The promulgation of the *Partidas,* of course, extended these laws to the Spanish colonies beyond the seas in Africa, Asia, and the New World, making them the most widely disseminated codex of laws in history. In Spanish America and in the Philippines the *Partidas* are still the common basic law. Indeed, Samuel Parsons Scott quotes jurisconsults and states: "In a considerable group of jurisdictions now under the sovereignty of the United States, civilized law began with the *Partidas,* or shortly before. Thus, in Louisiana the publication by Governor O'Reilly in 1769 of 'an extract from the whole body of Spanish law, with references to the books in which they are contained . . . followed from that moment by an uninterrupted observance of the Spanish law, has been received as an introduction of the Spanish code in all its parts'—i.e. the *Partidas*, which in fact were cited in the opinion of which the foregoing forms a part and for a long time thereafter in Louisiana Reports, besides being translated, as we have seen under the authority of the legislature of that State. Indeed, so late as 1924 the same Supreme Court devoted the major part of an opinion to a law of the *Partidas*, thus more than justifying the remarks of an eminent Louisiana lawyer: 'The *Partidas* are still worthy of careful study . . . some of its provisions remained as a part of the law of the state.' " And in Missouri, "We are informed," said the Missouri Supreme Court, "that the first printed book brought into this state, containing any Spanish law, was the *Partidas* and that event occurred later than the year 1820." [15]

The *Partidas*, also, remained in force in all the territory obtained from Mexico, and they likewise were in Texas until 1840, frequently cited in the reports of the Supreme Court there. In California they lasted until 1850 and were invoked in early cases in that state. The Supreme Court Records of the Philippines, which were not begun until 1901, contain in most of their volumes citations of the *Partidas*. Other cases could be cited in the Spanish American republics.

7. *The Content of the* Partidas

Alfonso decided to set up the laws in the *Partidas* in seven divisions because there were many precedents for this number— the Seven Liberal Arts, the seven years that Jacob served in order to marry Rachel, the Seven Joys of the Virgin and the Seven Sacraments of the Church. The seven *Partidas* may be listed by title as follows: I. LAW IN GENERAL; CANON LAW; II. PUBLIC LAW; GOVERNMENT AND ADMINISTRATION; III. PROCEDURE AND PROPERTY; IV. DOMESTIC RELATIONS, ETC.; V. OBLIGATIONS AND MARITIME LAW; VI. SUCCESSION; VII. CRIMES; EXEGESIS; GENERAL PRINCIPLES. Scott comments on the arrangement and points to some illogicality: "It is obvious enough now that the general matter in Books I and VII should have been combined. . . . It is also true that Books III and V should each have been divided and that the provisions relating to guardians in Book VI belong in Book IV. But we are not to expect either scientific accuracy or logical arrangement from thirteenth-century minds. In these particulars their work certainly excels the *Forum Judicum* and the wonder is that they did so well, even with the aid of their Roman models." [16]

So vast are the *Partidas* that it would require a long book to describe them in detail or, for that matter, even adequately. My procedure, therefore, will be to offer a short summary touching the major subject matter of each of the seven divisions, with portions translated from some of the more interesting sections, leaving legalistic treatment to such experts as Scott.

PARTIDA I is divided into twenty-four titles with five hundred and eighteen laws. It begins with a discussion of the nature of law, its divisions, functions, sources, who should make laws, their benefits, interpretation of law, observation, amendation, etc. Title II deals with usage of law, how customs are established, their force; the nature of *fueros*, how they are established and how abolished. Titles III and IV are concerned with the Trinity, the articles of the Catholic Faith, the Seven Sacraments and their virtues, penance, confession, etc.; mourning for the dead, the care of relics of saints, etc. Therefore, part of Title I of the first *Partida* and all the rest of its twenty-four titles are concerned with Catholic doctrine and the laws of the Church. But it was the first Title that helped to lead Sancho, Alfonso's son, and the nobles to revolt, for in it the King stresses the absolute authority of the monarch over all men and over all previous laws and *fueros*. Law XII of this Title reads: "AN EMPEROR OR KING MAY MAKE LAWS FOR THE PEOPLE OF HIS DOMINIONS, BUT NO ONE ELSE HAS THE POWER TO MAKE THEM WITH REGARD TO TEMPORAL MATTERS EXCEPT WHERE THEY DO SO WITH THEIR PERMISSION. THOSE THAT ARE MADE IN ANY OTHER WAY HAVE NEITHER THE NAME NOR THE EFFECT OF LAWS, NOR SHOULD THEY BE VALID AT ANY TIME."

Of special interest to students of literature is Title VI, Law 34, which will be presented here *in toto*, even though it is fairly long.

This single law reveals a great deal about drama in the thirteenth century, for in its provisions for the presentation of some forms of drama, and in its prohibitions against other types, we have the only definite facts available on dramatic productions in the thirteenth century, aside from the one extant play treated in Chapter 3. The law treats the virtues that priests should practice—charity, conducting services, etc., and continues with the material dealing with drama: "Nor should they [priests] throw dice, or play draughts, nor be connected with gamblers, or associate with them: nor enter wine-shops, unless compelled to do so on a journey, nor should they make scornful jest [the words in the original are *juegos de escarnio* meaning "jests" in the sense of "farcical plays," as will be seen further on] in order that people may visit them to hear them. If other men perform these things, ecclesiastics should not be present, because many evil speeches are uttered and indecencies committed there, nor should any such things take place in the churches; for we have previously declared that those who act in this manner should be dishonorably ejected from them, as the church of God is made to pray in, and not for the purpose of uttering scornful jests; for Our Lord Jesus Christ said in the Gospel that his house was called a house of prayer, and should not be made a den of thieves. There are certain representations, however, which ecclesiastics have a right to perform, for instance, that of the birth of Our Lord Jesus Christ, in which is shown how the angel appeared to the shepherds and told them that Jesus Christ was born, and also that of his appearance, and how the three kings of the Magi came to adore him, and the one relating to his resurrection, which shows that he was crucified, and arose on the third day. Representations of this kind which induce men to do good, and have devotion for the Faith, ecclesiastics can perform, and they are also beneficial, for they cause men to remember that the other events actually happened. These things should be done in an orderly way, and with great devotion, and should take place in large cities where there are archbishops or bishops, and either by their command, or by those of others who occupy their places; and they should not take place in villages, or in vile places, or for the sake of earning money by means of them." Hence it was legal, according to this *Partida*, to present miracle and mystery plays, those from the Nativity Cycle and the

Resurrection Cycle, but not to give *juegos de escarnio* or farces
or plays of an unseemly kind which were, of course, professional
and for which admission charges must have been made.

Partida II may be summarized briefly, at least as to tone and
aims, but certainly not in detail, for it contains thirty-one titles
and three hundred and fifty-six laws. This *Partida* discusses the
rights and duties of rulers as well as their obligations to their
subjects and of the subjects' duties and obligations to rulers. It
touches royal powers and privileges of the Castilian nobility and
the duties of all officials in the royal household, and all the qualities needed by such men to hold their offices, and even goes so
far as to discuss foreign nobility and the deportment of the ideal
ruler. Among its most interesting and delightful parts are those
dealing with the rearing of the children of kings. Title VII, Law
5, for example, reads: ". . . tutors should teach boys how to eat
and drink in a clean and polite manner; for, although this is something that no creature can avoid, nevertheless, men should not
do it in a coarse or awkward way: and especially does this apply
to the sons of kings, on account of the race from which they
spring, and the place which they will have to occupy, and from
the fact that others will have to follow their example. . . . They
declare that they should teach them to eat and drink in a well-
bred manner, not putting a second morsel into their mouths until
the first has been swallowed: for leaving out of consideration the
ill-breeding which will result from this, there is great danger that
they will be suddenly suffocated: and that they should not permit
them to grasp the morsel with all five fingers of their hand, for
fear they will make it too large. Also that they should not permit
them to eat inordinately with the entire mouth, but with a part
of it: for, by doing so they show themselves to be gluttons, which
is rather a characteristic of beasts than of men: and he who does
this cannot easily prevent what he is eating from dropping out of
his mouth, if he should desire to speak. . . . And they should
compel them to wash their hands before eating, that they may be
clean and free from what they have handled, for the cleaner food
is when it is eaten, the more beneficial it becomes. . . . They
declared, moreover, that they should not talk while they ate, because were they to do so, they must necessarily suffer loss in their
food, and be deficient as well with regard to what they dis-

cussed. Nor should they sing while they eat, as it is not the proper place for this, and it would appear that they did so rather through excitement of wine, than for any other reason. . . ."

Such discussions in a book of law seem strange indeed, until one remembers that the *Siete Partidas* were intended to guide the king's subjects as well as to dictate laws to them. The value to studies in contemporary manners and daily living is perfectly obvious.

This general section of the *Partidas* is followed by a treatise on the art of warfare, the custody of castles, war at sea, knights and their booty and captives. The section closes with a discussion of the *estudio general*, in Latin the *studium generale*, or university, and the courses it offers, the hiring, promotion and payment of professors, the rights of students, etc. In it one finds one of the best of all medieval discussions of higher education. In Title XXXI, we read of schools where the sciences are learned, and other matters concerning masters and pupils. Law 1 in this title is a good example of the detailed attention given by Alfonso and his legists to the matter of learning. This law is entitled WHAT A SCHOOL IS, HOW MANY KINDS THERE ARE, AND BY WHOSE COMMAND IT SHOULD BE ESTABLISHED. It reads: "A school is a union of masters and scholars, established in some locality with the will and design of teaching the sciences. There are two kinds of these; first, a general school, where there are masters of arts as, for instance, of grammar, logic, rhetoric, arithmetic, geometry, and astrology, and also where there are masters of ordinances, and lords of law. This school should be called a special school, which means one in which a master gives instruction to a few scholars in some town apart, and a school of this kind can be established by the order of a prelate, or the council of any locality."

The next law goes on to discuss the type of locale in which a school should be established: "The town where it is desired to establish a school should have pure air and beautiful environs in order that the masters who teach the sciences and the pupils who learn them may live there in health, and rest and take pleasure in the evening, when their eyes have become weary with study. . . . We declare that the citizens of the town where a school is situated should carefully protect its masters and pupils and everything belonging to them, and that no one should arrest or hinder the messengers who come to them from their homes on account of any debt that their parents, or any others of the countries where they are natives, may owe. . . . Whoever violates this law by taking their property by force, or by robbing them, shall pay four times the value of what is stolen, and where anyone wounds, dishonors, or kills any of them, he shall be punished without mercy, as a man who violates our truce, and the security which we have granted. . . ."

Law 11 discusses examinations that should be given students who desire to become professors: "Before they grant a license to anyone they should make a secret investigation, and ascertain if he who asks for it is a man of good reputation and of good habits, and he should also read some selections from the books of the science he desires to teach. If he has a competent understanding of the text and the commentary on the said science, a clear style, and a ready command of language to explain it, and, without hesitation, answers the questions and interrogations put to him, the honor of master should be publicly conferred upon him, he having first sworn to teach well and faithfully his branch of science, and that he neither gave, nor promised to give anything to those having authority to grant him a license, nor gave anything to any other person for them, to induce them to grant him the power of being master."

Even bookstores and the regulations for their management are discussed in Law 11: "Every general school, in order to be complete, must have booksellers, who should keep in their stores books which are good and legible and accurate both in text and in commentary, to be rented by pupils, to make new ones from, or to correct those which are already written. No one has the right to keep a shop or place of this kind without the permission of the rector of the university, and the latter, before he issues a license for this purpose, should first cause an examination to be made of the books. . . . Moreover, the rector should decide, with the advice of the school, how much the bookseller should receive for each book which he furnishes the pupil for the purpose of copying, or correcting their own books, and he should also require adequate security from the bookseller, binding him to take diligent and faithful care of all volumes given him to be sold, and not to commit fraud of any description."

PARTIDA III, containing thirty-two titles and six hundred and sixty-six laws, is a treatise on justice, judicial procedure, lawsuits, advocates and proxies, appeals, various types of proofs, etc. Included are matters treating seals and their validity and the duties and obligations of both royal and public scribes. One reads of minors being brought to court and of the prohibitions against minors; of slaves and the trials of slaves; of the right of the clergy to refuse to be hauled into court without the command of their superiors; rights of defendants and their obligation to speak in court when questioned; judges and their appointment, attorneys and their powers; summonses; of how ladies who are mistresses of their own houses, or young ladies, or other women living honorably at home cannot be summoned to appear personally before a judge; that a woman cannot be summoned before a judge who has attempted to violate her or marry her without her consent; oaths and the swearing in of witnesses (this differs for Jews and Christians); evidence, interrogation, number of witnesses in a case; bills of sale, letters of safe conduct; guardians and wills; appeals, restitution, property rights (for example, of how he who finds gold, pearls, or precious stones on the sea shore obtains ownership of them); or to whom a deer belongs which has been wounded by one party and taken by another (the one who first comes into possession of it, even though he may not have wounded it, is entitled to keep the deer).

PARTIDA IV, with its twenty-seven titles and two hundred and fifty-six laws, discusses marriage and betrothal, adoptions, paternal rights; slavery and freedom, vassalage and fiefs, etc. Some of the details are extremely revealing of the way of life in those times and are most interesting to read. Parents ought not to betroth their daughters if the girls are not present to agree; we read of who can marry and who cannot; or what punishment the king has established to be inflicted upon those who marry women clandestinely without the knowledge of their parents; of annulments, the marriage of slaves, of impotence and of how it prevents marriage; of persons who are bewitched in such a way that they cannot have sexual intercourse; and of the distinction between those who are bewitched and those who are cold by nature.

Law 6, on the ages of people permitted to marry, is of interest. "Males and females can be betrothed after they are seven years of age, because then they begin to possess intelligence, and are old enough to be content with a betrothal; and if any persons are betrothed before they arrive at this age, or their relatives contract such a betrothal in their names, one or both of them being under seven years of age, none of their acts will be valid; except where they have passed this age, and are content with what they have done, and agree to it, for in this case the betrothal will be valid. . . . In order for a marriage to be contracted, the male must be fourteen years of age and the female twelve, and where any persons are married before that time, it will not be a marriage, but a betrothal, except when they are so near it that they are already fitted for carnal union; for the knowledge and the ability for the performance of this make up for the deficiency of age."

Concubinage is discussed freely in Law 1 of Title XIV: "Every woman who from her birth has been free from all servitude and has never been a slave, is called in Latin *ingenua mulier*. A woman of this kind can be accepted as a concubine according to law, whether she belongs to a low family, or was born in some vile place, and whether she makes an evil use of her body or not. The name *barragana* is derived from two words; one of them Arabic, which means 'outside,' and the other Christian, which means 'to gain,' and these two words, when united, mean something earned outside the rules of the church. . . .[11] Law 3 of Title III tells how long a woman can be pregnant after the death of her husband without being accused of adultery; Law 5 deals with the birth of monsters: "Creatures born of women, and who are not formed as human beings, as where they have the heads or limbs of beasts, should not be considered children. For which reason neither their fathers nor mothers are bound to make them heirs of their property, nor are they entitled to it, although they may be proved to be heirs. But where a creature is born with the form of a man, although he may have too many, or too few limbs, this does not prevent him from inheriting the property of his father or mother, or other relatives."

PARTIDA V, which contains fifteen titles and three hundred seventy-five laws, is a treatise on commercial law, fairs, markets, contracts and debts, the merchant marine; on gifts, titles, fraudulent sales (as of hidden blemishes of animals); on tolls and the penalties for leaving the road to avoid them; on fishermen who make signal fires at night for the purpose of causing shipwrecks; on partnership, promises, bail, etc. Title XIV, Law 17 reads: "Where a minor over seven years of age and under fourteen, on his own responsibility, makes a contract, binding himself to pay the debt of another without the consent of his guardian; the first contract is annulled by such a renewal, and the party who made it will be released, so that he will not afterwards be bound to pay the debt, nor will the minor either, if he does not desire to do so. The party who renewed the obligation with a minor of this kind must assume the blame, because said minor has no authority to make a contract to his own injury."

PARTIDA VI, with its nineteen titles and two hundred and eighty-two laws, deals with inheritance and with wills and testaments of all kinds. Some of the titles are interesting enough to set down verbatim: A FATHER CAN DISINHERIT HIS SON IF HE BECOMES A MOOR, A JEW, OR A HERETIC (Title VII, Law 7); A PARTY WHO EMANCIPATES A SLAVE OF HIS WHO IS UNDER AGE, SHALL BE THE GUARDIAN OF HIM AND HIS PROPERTY (Title XVI, Law 10). Title XVI, Law 16, A GUARDIAN MUST TEACH MINORS TO READ AND WRITE, is interesting: "A guardian should exert himself to induce the minor of whom he has charge to acquire good habits, and he should also teach him to read and write and, after this, so instruct him that he may learn and practice the occupation most suitable for him, according to the character, wealth, or power which he may possess. He should also take care of, and provide for him, furnishing him with food, clothing, and other necessaries, as he thinks his duty requires him to do, although being careful to do this in proportion to the property which he receives from him."

PARTIDA VII, with thirty-four titles and two hundred and forty-three laws, is a tract on criminal law and its penalties and on certain classes of people like Jews and Moors and heretics. One finds that slaves cannot accuse another person (Title I, Law

3), or reads of accusations and how they are to be made and by whom; of treason and its punishment; of combats and trial by combat; of men who wrongly castrate others and deserve the penalty for homicide; of dishonor and its causes and penalties; of violence, robbery, larceny, theft; of physicians who must make reparation to their patients who are harmed by treatment (Title XV, Law 9). The owner of a horse or other domestic animal is required to pay for any damage committed by it (Law 22). "What Penalty a Christian Deserves Who Becomes a Jew" (Title VII, Law 7) tells us that "Where a Christian is so unfortunate as to become a Jew, we order that he shall be put to death just as if he had become a heretic; and we decree that his property shall be disposed of in the same way that we stated should be done with that of heretics."

Some punishments were harsh indeed. Title XXXIII, Law 4 is one of these: "A citizen or resident of a town or village who offers an insult to God or to Holy Mary, for the first offense shall lose the fourth part of his property; for the second, the third part; and for the third, the half; and if, after the third time, he repeats the offense, he shall be banished from the country. If he is a man of inferior rank who has nothing, he shall receive fifty lashes for the first offense; for the second, he shall be branded on the lips with a hot iron on which is the letter "B"; and the third time that he does this, his tongue shall be cut out."

Belief and superstitions may be studied with profit in this *Partida*. Title XXIII, Laws 1, 2, 3 are revealing, but number 3 is perhaps the most interesting: WHO CAN PROSECUTE IN COURT THE DIVINERS, SORCERERS, AND SWINDLERS AND WHAT PENALTY THEY DESERVE: "Anyone of the people can prosecute in court the diviners, sorcerers, and swindlers whom we have mentioned in the laws of this Title; and if they should be convicted by witnesses, or by their own confessions of having committed any of the above-mentioned offenses, contrary to our prohibition, they shall suffer death for this reason; and those who knowingly conceal them in their houses shall be banished from our dominions for life. Such, however, as practice enchantments or anything else with good intentions as, for instance, to cast out devils from the bodies of men; or to dissolve the spell cast over husband and wife so that they are unable to

[132]

perform their marital duties; or to turn aside a cloud from which hail or a fog is descending, that it may not injure the crops; or to kill locusts or insects which destroy grain or vines; or for any other beneficial purpose similar to these, cannot be punished, but we decree that they shall be rewarded for it."

Alfonsine law, then, and most especially the *Siete Partidas*, represents a turning point in legal history in Spain and reveals that in still another area of learning this King was far ahead of his times and that he realized it. When sociologists make a complete and careful study of the content of these remarkable laws, they will be able to understand a very great deal about the way men lived in the Middle Ages.

CHAPTER 8

Translations from Arabic: Scientific Works and Books on Games

I Scientific Works

AMONG the nonliterary books produced under the patronage of the Learned King are many translations from Arabic, most especially from books of science and to a lesser extent from those which deal with games, particularly with the eastern game of chess. Some question might well arise in the mind of the reader as to the propriety of including such works in this study, owing to their technical nature. But the fame of Alfonso X rests to no small degree upon the books of science and upon the scientific investigations and experiments carried out under his supervision: the complete investigation, therefore, must accord some treatment to this aspect of the King's interests. The effect of such writings upon true literature cannot be established with great ease, but it is only just to state that those who gave some time to belles-lettres in his own century, and in subsequent ages, drew at least occasionally upon these books.

Royal interest and sponsorship of the sciences was no new thing in Spain when Alfonso ascended the throne and began his patronage in earnest. He was again following the ancient tradition of Spanish kings who had preceded him. His own father, King Ferdinand, had done much to stimulate the arts, letters, and sciences, but, occupied as he was during most of his reign with almost constant warfare with the Moors, he had not been able to devote the time he would have liked to such peaceful pursuits. He did, however, plant the seeds of these interests in the mind of his son, and he must have felt assured of their later burgeoning. But even before the time of Ferdinand other Spanish monarchs had espoused the sciences. Alfonso VI (1072–1109), who captured Toledo in 1085, knew the importance of the Moorish universities in that city and permitted them to survive and function. Alfonso VII (1126–57) had gone even further, for he had founded there about 1130, a school of translators whose primary duty was the rendering of scientific works from Arabic into Spanish. His was a very beneficial service to learning, for with it he began the long period of channeling most of the then known eastern scientific knowledge into Spanish and through Spanish to much of western Europe.

Most of the translators of this time and later, and of course this includes those of Alfonso X, were Jews, generally Sephardic Jews, the most highly educated and cultured in the world. Sephardic Jews had lived in Toledo for generations, some say even before the coming of the Moors, and had served their Moorish masters in many learned capacities. It would be interesting to turn aside here to discuss these great Arabic universities, staffed by learned Moslems and Jews, but space will not permit, and, in any case, the reader has at his disposal in many libraries excellent treatments of these matters. It can only be said that such institutions had existed in most of the cities under Moorish domination. The Spanish Jews were bilingual, speaking Arabic and Spanish, and their scholars and rabbis often could even read Greek and Hebrew, and of course, Latin, which all learned people found it necessary to master.

Still another source of patronage of the sciences came from members of the hierarchy of the Spanish Church. Among the greatest of these had been Raimundo, second Archbishop of Toledo (1125–51), whose efforts to stimulate the sciences in his see had been eminently successful. Famous as a scientist himself, and as a man who contributed bountifully to study and all branches of scientific activity, he created a center of culture and a great library in which were archived many eastern books as well as many written by Spanish Moors and Spanish Jews, or translated by these men from foreign languages. Archbishop Raimundo wanted to rid the Peninsula of the infidel, and lent strong support to Alfonso VII in his wars, but at the same time he wished to retain all that Moorish culture and learning could contribute. Working under his aegis, a school of scholars grew up known as the College of Toledan Translators, which soon became famous, attracting the learned from other parts of Spain and from far beyond the Pyrenees. Among these were Archdeacon Domingo Gonzálvez of Segovia, Rabbi Abraham Benezra; a famous astrologer named El Toleitoli; and the Spanish Jew, Juan Hispalense. At Toledo, Gerard of Cremona learned Arabic and became the greatest of all the translators, and Michael Scott, Alfred of Sareschel, Gerard of Sabionetta, and Herman the German worked.

Ecclesiastical patronage continued well beyond this period; indeed, well beyond the reign of Alfonso X. Church-supported schools of translators, then, survived from Moorish times and were perpetuated by the Church, or new schools of translators were founded. In Tarragona, Hugh of Santalla gathered translators about him; in Huesca the converted Jew, Pedro Alfonso, translated his famous *Disciplina Clericalis*, "Scholar's Guide," which would later serve as one of the sources of the *Decameron* and of Spanish works as well.

Alfonso X, who quickly established a group of translators in his palace at Toledo after he was crowned, had many collaborators in the production of his books on the sciences. A number of their names are known, and in a good many cases we can even state with some certainty which scholar, or pair of scholars, translated which Arabic scientific treatise. Alfonso had at his court, under his royal patronage and support, John of Messina, Fernando de Toledo, Maestre Jacome Ruiz, John of Cremona, Lope de Loaysa, Archdeacon of Toledo, Martínez de Zamora, and Gil de Zamora, later to be Preceptor of Prince Sancho, Alfonso's son. Among Jewish scholars subsidized by the Learned King were Judah ben Moses ha-Cohen, Samuel ha-Levi Abulafia, Isaac ibn Sid ha-Hazzan, Abraham Alfaquín de Toledo, Judah-Aben-Mosca, the personal physician of the King, and Rabbi Zag Aben Cayut, often spoken of as Rabiçag. From the names mentioned, it will be seen that Italians, Spaniards, and Spanish Jews made up the greater part of the translators. In discussing the work of these translators, it should be noted that in most cases a Jew and a Christian collaborated. This practice was old in Spain, and the Learned King merely followed what had proved successful before his times. Two experts, it was believed, each a specialist in his own language, whether Arabic or Spanish, could produce a better translation than one scholar who was less well-versed in two tongues.

1. *The Alfonsine Tables*

I shall not attempt to offer a detailed treatment of all the various translations from the Arabic, as most of these are extremely technical and can hardly be understood by any save students of the history of science. But a few of the most influential should be discussed, at least in general terms.[1] The most important and influential in Alfonso's own time, and in later periods as well, was the book called the *Tablas Alfonsinas,* "Alfonsine Tables," which offered detailed charts and diagrams of the movements of the planets. The *Tables* of Alfonso were translations of the findings of the Cordovan astronomer al-Zarqali, but included many changes, corrections, and additions made as the result of scientific investigations carried out at Alfonso's command. At Toledo during the first months of 1260, Alfonso and his scientists made careful observations of the latitudes and longitudes of fourteen stars. They chose Toledo because it was the center of the realm and because its skies were clear and free of mist and fog. The experiments were carried out on the plain and in the Palaces of Galiana, which Ballesteros identifies as to locale.[2] Apparently the experiments covered the period from 1252 to 1262 and were ended on May 12 of the latter year. All the best scientific minds available were present. The cost of such activities was not small —indeed, it must have been prohibitive—and much note was taken of such seemingly unnecessary expenditure. Such criticism no doubt did much to magnify the remarkable fame enjoyed by the *Alfonsine Tables.* In revised form, written by John of Lignières in Paris in the fourteenth century, these *Tables* influenced scientific thinking in a very great part of western Europe well into the Renaissance. To the average person of Alfonso's times, such imposing matters as the movements of the planets and the instruments used in computing these movements smacked of the awe-inspiring and even of the dark arts. The *Tables,* then, were responsible for much of the King's fame as a man of mystery and a sage. These *Tables* concern themselves primarily with eclipses and the measurement of time; they are complex, technical, and somewhat dry to those not interested in the development of such matters. Perhaps the most ideal and graphic way to convey some idea of the content and presentation of the *Tablas Alfonsinas* would be a short sample in translation from this work.[3]

CHAPTER I. HOW ONE IS TO DETERMINE THE ERA IN WHICH THESE TABLES ARE SET UP AND ITS BEGINNING

"All the eras which are manifest in the nations, and used, old and new, are begun with some one event which took place. And the people of that realm honored that event and called it the beginning of their years, and took account of the said happening so that the fame of it would endure and would not be forgotten for long ages.

"And for this reason all the eras are set up since the world began until now. The Greeks began their eras from King Alexander, taking the year in which he was born, because he was a very powerful king, and one whom they greatly esteemed. Thus their era was called the Era of Alexander.

"Likewise the Romans took the year in which Caesar began to rule, and named their era after him, because he was a king whom they honored very much. And this is the era which is now used, and it is named the Era of Caesar."

The chapter continues with the Arabic Era and the Persian Era, and states, to the modern reader's surprise, ". . . and we see that in this period of ours a notable and honored event took place and of as much greatness as all those of the past. And this is the rule of our lord King Alfonso, who excelled all kings in wisdom, and learning and law, goodness, piety and nobility. And on this account we deem it fitting to establish the beginning of the era in that year when this noble king began to reign so that this era may be used and made manifest, just as the other eras before it were used and made manifest, so that the fame of this noble king may endure and remain forever. And we establish the beginning of this aforementioned year as the beginning of this era, and we give it the name of the Alfonsine Era."

The scientific works, translations from the Arabic, may be logically divided for convenience into three categories: (1) books of astronomical content; (2) those of astrological content; and (3) those which deal with magic. Representative of the last

[138]

variety is a book without title, without date, and with no statement that it was prepared at the behest of the King; but it bears
a close resemblance to the other books he sponsored, ". . . and
the contents," writes Evelyn Proctor, "appear to correspond to
part of the Latin *Liber Picatrix* which has survived in manuscripts of the fifteenth century and later, and which is stated to
be based on a vernacular translation made at Alfonso's command
in 1256." [4]

2. *The Books of the Wisdom of Astronomy*

Another famous and important work, rivaling the fame of the
Tablas, is really a series of treatises or books put together under
one title and known as *Los Libros del Saber de Astronomía,* "The
Books of the Wisdom of Astronomy." All fifteen of these treatises
were translated from Arabic books written from the ninth into
the twelfth century. Some of these treatises were translated early
in Alfonso's reign—or as early as 1255 through 1259—but they
were not assembled under their single title until after 1276. "It
is, indeed, probable," Evelyn Proctor states, "that most of these
translations were undertaken early in the reign in connexion with
the compilation of the *Tablas,* since the works deal with instruments which could be used in making observations, although
some of them were revised at the time that the collection was
made." [5] These books revise the astronomical system devised by
Ptolemy. Modern readers find them interesting only as curiosities,
but those who care to observe the evolution of the science of
astronomy find them valuable. They are complex and filled with
precise mathematical rules for various studies of the stars, their
movements, and the constellations, and they offer carefully explained plans and methods for the construction of the instruments necessary for such measurements and observations.

As in the case of the *Tablas,* translation is the best method of
imparting something of the tone and character of the *Books of
the Wisdom of Astronomy.*

CHAPTER LXV.   OF KNOWING WHETHER THERE WILL
BE AN ECLIPSE OF THE SUN IN THAT MONTH OR NOT

"If you wish to know this in the celestial sphere, verify the
latitude of the moon on the twenty-seventh day of the lunar

month, and if you should find the moon on that day with no latitude, and that its degree agrees with its greatest ascendancy in the ring of midday, you will know that the sun will be eclipsed in that month without any doubt. And if you find the moon in latitude on that day, learn how great it is and in what part, and if the latitude of the moon would be northerly and if it were one degree and thirty-seven minutes or less, you will likewise know that the sun will be eclipsed in that month. And if this northerly latitude should be more than one degree and thirty-seven minutes, the sun will not be eclipsed in that month. And if the latitude of the moon were southerly and it were of forty-seven minutes or less, the sun will be eclipsed in that month. And if it were more than forty-seven minutes, the sun will not be eclipsed in that month."

Although Alfonso was never able to spend long periods of time in Toledo, he nonetheless visited the city often for periods of short duration and must have often consulted his scholars and translators. Ballesteros and Evelyn Proctor give long lists of the works and of their translators, but as these lists mention the titles found in the various treatises which made up the *Libros del Saber de Astronomía*, I shall not repeat them. Let it suffice to say here that Alfonso apparently decided what books needed to be translated and who should make the translations. Afterward he edited, that is, read, corrected, abbreviated, and enlarged, and at times ordered whole treatises retranslated. This last is notably observable in the *Libro del Saber de Astronomía*, for three of its books have been translated at least twice, and one of them, the *Libro de la Açafena*, was translated originally at Toledo in 1256, but was later translated in Burgos "better and more completely."

Moreover, Alfonso, who was a teacher at heart, caused diagrams and charts to be placed in some of his books and described in great detail how these were to appear as to form and color. One can compare the descriptions of the diagrams with the actual charts and find that the King's instructions were carried out to the letter. His part in the works, then, cannot be disputed.

3. *Books of Astrology*

Astrology was also one of the interests of Alfonso X, as has been stated above. If this should seem strange, when one con-

siders the truly scientific efforts of this King, one should consider
the times and the backgrounds of such beliefs. Astrology had
been treated for ages in the East as a science, or if not quite an
exact science, at least a body of knowledge which belonged to
the family of the sciences. Its ties with astronomy were close,
and at times it is difficult to draw a line of demarcation between
the two. And astrology, as was not so much the case with astronomy, had firm ties indeed with medieval literature. Its influence
upon contemporary, and even later writing, is strong. Some, like
Don Juan Manuel, Alfonso's nephew, for example, scoffed at it
and refused to believe in the prediction of the future through
horoscopes and stargazing. With others one cannot be as certain,
especially when one has to deal with the *Libro de Buen Amor,*
"The Book of Good Love," of Juan Ruiz, Archpriest of Hita. My
personal feeling is that this enigmatic and unfathomable ecclesiastic wrote tongue-in-cheek when he brought astronomy into
his immortal book, but with him it is never safe to make categori-
cal statements. At any rate, the Learned King seems to have believed in the influence of the stars in the lives of mortals, and his
books on the subject make fascinating reading. Unfortunately,
there has been an incomplete survival of all of the treatises which
made up the collection, *Libro de las Formas e de Las Ymagenes
que Son en los Cielos e de las Vertudes e de las Obras que Salen
dellas en los Cuerpos que Son dyuso del Cielo e de la Luna,* "Book
of the Forms and Images Which Are in the Heavens and of the
Virtues and of the Results Which Come From Them into the
Bodies Which Are Beneath the Heavens and the Moon." We can
know most of them only through the titles which are extant in
the table of contents of the treatises in the great book. Preceding
the table of contents is a statement that the treatises were begun
in 1276 at the express command of Alfonso X and completed in
1279.

Of the eleven tracts or component parts, the first is a lapidary
ascribed to a certain Abolays; this book today is in the Library
of the Escorial.[6] Actually, it is not a single treatise on the lapidary science, but four separate lapidaries; the last of these is
mentioned as having been written by one Aben Quich. Two of
the other three are not ascribed to any author, but since Abolays
had been called the author of the first treatise in the volume, it

is assumed that he wrote the others saving, of course, that ascribed to Aben Quich. The first of these, assigned to Abolays, deals for the most part with the scientific and medicinal properties of stones and gems and the regions of the earth from which these derive. The second and third concern themselves, on the other hand, with the magical virtues and powers of the stones. Evelyn Proctor reveals that there is some doubt as to the place of the lapidaries in the *Libro de las Formas,* but goes on to say that ". . . whatever may be the relationship between the lost *Libro de las Formas* and the extant lapidaries, one thing at least seems certain—both the Escorial manuscripts are royal manuscripts and emanated from the scriptorium attached to Alfonso's chamber." [7]

The *Lapidary* is one of the most beautiful of medieval books and, fortunately, has been printed in facsimile with all its brilliant color and illumination. And although it is a rare book today, it can be found in most of our larger civic and university libraries. Only the *Cantigas de Santa María* surpasses it in artistic excellence.

The attractive book reveals that the lapidary science, along with which it is closely enough related to be placed as a part of the *Libro de las Formas,* was taken seriously. Medieval man believed in the virtues of stones; that, for example, birthstones could exert an influence on men's lives, and that the action of the stars upon these stones was powerful and important in mortal affairs. Even medical doctors set great store by stones. They pulverized many as medication for their patients and recommended that people wear others as amulets against diseases and other dangers. According to the Prologue of the first of the three treatises ascribed to Abolays, it is stated that he translated from Chaldean into Arabic. We are justified in thinking that "Chaldean" meant in those times "Syriac."

On the first page of the first treatise of Abolays, just before that part of the page that is the Index, appears a miniature in vivid colors representing Alfonso and his scholars, translators, and scientists. In black-letter text is the statement that the book has been translated "from the books of the ancient philosophers," and that it was rendered into Spanish in the Era 1314, that is, according to Christian computation, the year 1276,[8] the twenty-fifth year of the Learned King's reign. It was transcribed at the command of "the much exalted and honored Don Alfonso, lover of sciences and learning, by the Grace of God, King of Castile and León, Toledo, Galicia, Seville, Córdova, Murcia, Jaén and Algarve." The over-all *Lapidary*, and it seems safe to term it thus as one title rather than as four separate titles, is divided into twelve parts, each to represent one of the signs of the Zodiac.

Each of the twelve divisions is headed by an elaborate design, surrounded by its corresponding constellations, which are said to influence "all earthly bodies," for if one is to believe the *Lapidary*, a mysterious waxing and waning of the virtues of stones and plants occurs as the stars alter their positions in the heavens. The greater divisions are further divided into many short chapters, and most of these contain full-colored illuminated miniatures, much smaller than those in the *Cantigas*, since few occupy whole pages as do those in that collection of miracles of the Virgin. In these minia-tures one is able to observe much of medieval life and customs. The stones are described, and those who mine them or gather them from streams or from the sea are depicted at work. Charts associated with zodiacal signs indicate the parts of the bodies of men and of animals affected by the various stones. Not all of the names of the stones are in Spanish or in Latin, for many bear Arabic names, and since these names belonged to the Middle Ages and have not survived in modern Arabic, it is not possible today to identify all of them. Some three hundred and sixty stones, pre-cious and nonprecious, are listed, and to many the most fantastic virtues imaginable are ascribed.

One reads, for example, of "the stone of sleep," which is red, transparent and difficult to shatter, impervious to flame and which glows at night so that "those who live on the Isle of Ali-cuas, near the Sea of Alcuzum [the Red Sea], on whose shores the stone is found, when they see a light shining at their feet in the night, stoop and pick up the stone of sleep." [9] The *Lapidary* tells us that this stone of sleep was highly prized by physicians, and especially by surgeons, because it caused a restful and peaceful slumber, after which the patient awakened clear of mind and refreshed and rested in body. Therefore, ". . . it is much used for the wounded so that for awhile, they may forget all pain." This powerful stone, when used as medicine, had to be

[143]

taken with care and only under the scrutiny of a doctor who knew its virtues. "One single drachma of it is enough to induce three entire days and three entire nights of uninterrupted slumber, and even then, if the sleeper is not awakened by one who understands the virtue of the stone of sleep and knows how to give the sleeper his full release, he will turn over and sleep again." [10]

Another chapter, entitled ABOUT THE STONE WHICH IS CALLED THE DIAMOND, is too long to quote here in its entirety, but it is of such interest that I have translated parts of it.

"The Sign of Taurus [the Bull] is the second among the twelve signs of the Zodiac we have mentioned. It is divided into thirty degrees and a kindred stone corresponds to each degree; and it is from these that it holds its virtues, as will be explained as follows. The stone called *Mex* in Arabic and diamond in Latin is the first of these stones. By nature this stone is cold and dry in the fourth degree. It takes its origin in the River known as Borabicem, which flows through the land called Boracim. But it crystallizes into stone only in a land that has six months of continual daylight and six months of continual darkness. No man has ever visited the land where this river begins, for there are many serpents and other beasts dangerous in diverse ways, and there are also vipers which can kill a man by merely looking at him. For these reasons men do not dare to travel to that place. . . .

"When the river is in flood, many small tributaries and canals branch away from it, and these carry the stones along. And again, where the river originates there are many large stones and many small ones. Of these, some are of transparent and yet darkish hue, reminding one of brass; others are pale green or pale yellow, but the best are those that resemble clear glass . . ." [11]

Diamonds could be pulverized by wrapping them in sheets of lead and striking them with a mallet. "If a little of this powder is mixed with some other material and administered to a man suffering from bladder stone, the stone is quickly destroyed and the patient cured. Some take a small fragment of diamond and attach it to a thin piece of iron and apply it to a man who is suffering from a stone in the genital organs in such a way that the diamond touches the diseased part. At once the stone is broken up, but it should only be applied in cases where recovery is very doubtful." [12]

A strange belief as to the poisonous qualities of diamonds is given. "The diamond is also very poisonous on account of the venomous beasts which breed where the stone is gathered. As the stones are invariably square in shape and have sharp outlines, they scrape against these venomous creatures and are thus impregnated with their poison. Therefore, when a diamond it taken into the mouth and held there for a while it destroys the teeth and causes them to drop out. It does even worse damage: if a man takes the weight of a drachma and pulverizes it with the shell of lead, as above mentioned, and causes a man to drink it, that man will die." [13]

Of still more fantastic nature is the belief that diamonds have somewhat supernatural powers, even more astonishing than their medicinal ones. ". . . those that carry it are straightway cured, move swiftly, and can do anything that requires courage and daring. The fiery star which is located in the right muscle of the arm of the One Who Looks up with Attention, and the Other One, which is just above the head of the same figure, hold the power over this stone, and it is from these that it obtains its virtue. When these stars are in mid-heaven, the stone exercises its greatest power."

Intriguing is the "stone that flees away from wine." In the *Lapidary* it has no other name, but Ptolemy is quoted as having been an authority on it, and he was regarded in the Middle Ages as one of the great savants. The "stone that flees from wine," found on an island in the Sea of Alcusun, where strange trees grow bearing fruit shaped like the figure of a woman suspended by the hair of the head, was, according to the *Lapidary*, a very valuable stone, because it was clear and beautiful and was used by kings for their crowns; but the chief characteristic was its propensity to jump away from wine for which it has great abhorrence. ". . . when it is burned, its ashes will retain the beautiful color of the stone and will have such a power that if the ashes are placed in a barrel of wine, the latter will be changed into a liquid the color of clear water, no matter how strong the wine had been." [14] It was further believed that this stone protected people who wore it from giving away to devilish imaginations and kept them from being afraid of the dark.

A few further brief excerpts will suffice: ". . . the emerald is a remedy for all deadly poisons and for wounds and the bites of venomous beasts; take one drachma and pulverize it and give it in wine or in water to a man who has been poisoned and he will not perish, nor lose his hair, nor will his skin peel off"; and ". . . if one has an emerald engraved with the figure of a man or of a lion, he may travel from court to court with no fear of danger, fully aware that he will be well received by princes and great men"; [15] another stone, also found in the Red Sea is "the stone of the hermit, which had the most remarkable virtue imaginable, for ". . . men use it in strings of beads or have it set into rings, so that when they wear it they may escape the wiles of women; and therefore in ancient times wise men gave it to hermits and pious men and to all who took the vow of celibacy"; [16] he who carries a ruby will drive away any kind of sadness whatever; Carnelian "is good for lawyers, for it strengthens their voices and endows them with the power to plead their cases without fear, but only when certain constellations and planets are in ascendancy, for at other times it makes them sad and downcast"; another stone, called *stopaza,* of obvious identity, had the power of sticking to snakes and other reptiles so that they could be caught; green jasper, under certain conditions, caused strife; a stone known as *zayetanizes* rendered people immune to the bites of insects and beetles; still another "flies away from honey"; and there was a stone that attracted gold as the magnet attracts iron.[17]

The book of Alfonso's may have been the first in the vernacular to place eastern gem lore at the disposal of medieval Europeans. It supplemented the already known lapidaries handed down from Greece and Rome and colored the imagination of medieval writers, scientists and, of course, fortune-tellers and soothsayers.

A few other titles should at least be listed, although they are technical in the extreme and will not be read by any but a few scholars. Evelyn Proctor discusses these as follows. "There are also translations of a number of separate works: an astronomical compendium in Ibn al-Haitam, the canons of al-Battani, Ptolemy's *Quadripartitum* (which served the Middle Ages as a textbook of astrology) together with the commentary of 'Ali Iben

'Abi-l-Rijal (Abenragel), entitled in Castilian *El Libro de los Juicios de las Estrellas,* and another astrological work by a certain 'Ubaid Allah' called in its Castilian dress, *El Libro de las Cruces.* The Castilian translations of the *Quadripartitum* and of the compendium of Ibn al-Haitam have perished, but are known from Latin translations made from the Castilian. . . ." [18]

Two translations of the *Libro de los Juicios de las Estrellas* were made into Latin at the behest of the Learned King with the title *Liber Magnus et Completus de Iudiciis Astrologiae,* "Great and Complete Book of the Judgements of Astrology." Such were the books on magic, astronomy, astrology, the sciences, and stones and related subjects. All these matters interested Alfonso, and all found in him an ardent supporter whose bountiful purse made their translations possible. Spain and Christian Europe were for centuries to read these treatises. They must, therefore, be considered a keystone in the framework of the history of science in the West.

II *Books on Games*

The Learned King died in 1284, but even in his last troubled years he continued to have books written. The one entitled *Libro de Ajedrez, Dados y Tablas,* "Book of Chess, Dice and Backgammon," was finished in Seville in 1283 and is one of the last, if not the very last, of his productions. Today it is regarded as the most important medieval treatise on these games, and especially on chess. Interesting manuscripts, illuminated and in wonderful color, are preserved in the Escorial. Like other books which treat of oriental subjects, this book was translated from Arabic, but it is more than a mere translation; it represents an advance and improvement upon all eastern books on chess—in detail, additions, and in the discussion of games of chess not found in earlier works. The miniatures depict each variety of the game of chess and show the players, most of whom are orientals, although by no means all, for one sees European men and women playing, and even monks and children.

The pictures are not rendered with the skill and attractiveness of the ones portrayed in the *Cantigas de Santa María* or the *Lapidary,* but they are well worth careful study. For the most part they simply portray the players and the chess, dice or back-gammon board, drawn in such a way that the boards appear to be perpendicular to the viewer, a device for showing what was on the board. Viewed from the normal horizontal position, the viewer could not see the individual pawns, bishops, etc., and could not follow the pictorial presentation of the games described with great care in the text. Other pictures show factories where dice and chessmen were made in what can best be described as an assembly line. Some workers with adzes cut squares of bone for the dice; others bore the holes and add black stain to the dots; still others stand by to polish and perfect. The drills, the work tables, the inks are all clearly depicted.

Alfonso seemed definitely interested in providing games for his subjects to play. In the Prologue to the *Libro de Ajedrez* we read a revealing passage:

"Because God wished that all variety of joy should reside in men naturally, so that they could endure cares and hardships when these beset them, men therefore investigated many ways by which they could obtain this joy." [19]

He goes on to explain that many prefer such sports as jousting, hunting, throwing quoits, and the like, but states that more sedentary recreations are a necessity also. The detail in which this is explained shows again a mind that concentrated upon the problems at hand, even the psychological problems of tedium and boredom.

"The other games which are played while sitting are such as playing chess and backgammon and dice, and other games of diverse kinds. Therefore, all these games are very good, each in the time and place which befit it, for these games played while sitting can be played at any time, by night as well as by day, and because women who do not ride and are housebound can play them, and likewise men who are old and weak or those who take their pleasures apart and privately so as not to have annoyances or grief, or those who are in another's power, as in prison or captivity, or those who travel upon the sea; and in general all those who endure bad weather, so that they cannot ride or go hunting or anywhere else, and have perforce to remain indoors and seek some varieties of games with which they may entertain themselves and not be in tedium."

[148]

CAPITULO DE QUAL MANERA DEBEN TOMAR CON LOS JUEGOS DEL AJEDREZ

"The taking of chessmen by one another is in this manner: the king takes, in all the houses in which we say that he can move, any other chessman of the other side which is there."

CAPITULO DE LAS AVANTAIAS DE LOS TREBEIOS DEL ACEDREX

"The advantages which chessmen have over one another are great, for the king is empowered so that he can capture all chessmen and none is able to take him. And this is like the case of the [actual] king who is able to carry out justice upon all those who deserve it, but for this none of them can lay a hand upon him so as to arrest him nor wound him nor kill him, although he may wound or arrest or kill. But they are able to take vengeance [in the game, it is meant] upon him in three ways: by forcing him to go out of the house in which he rests, or by preventing his entering the house which he wishes to enter, and by not permitting him to take what he wishes.

"The bishop has likewise great advantage because he guards the king at close range more than the other chessmen, and is better than the pawns because he has more squares in which he can go and take than they have. And likewise he guards and moves both backwards and forwards, which the pawns cannot do . . . The horse [knight] has greater advantages than all the chessmen save the rook, because the player who knows well how to play with the horse, moving him from the first house of one side of the board, will take as many chessmen as there may be in all the houses of the board, which are sixty-three minus the house in which he stands, for never does he fail to take, according as he moves."

Aside from the usual game of chess with all its intricate moves, described detail by detail, there are other games in which only certain chessmen are permitted to appear; moreover, there are such games as Great Chess and Chess of the Ten Houses, and we are told that there is a game of chess in which one throws dice to indicate which or how many moves he may take; and there are games of chess and of backgammon which are played by astronomical indications.

III Mohammed's Ladder

Students of literature will continue to contemplate this strange book, actually nonextant in its originally translated form in Castilian, because it seems definitely to foreshadow the *Divine Comedy* of Dante. Fortunately, an Old French version made from Alfonso's translation from the Arabic survives—the sole representative of the Alfonsine work. It rests in the Bodleian Library and bears the title *Livre de Leschiele Mahomet*, "Mohammed's Ladder." The Prologue of this book states that it was translated into Spanish at the behest of Alfonso X, "King of the Romans," which alludes, of course, to the fact that he once had aspired to be emperor of the Holy Roman Empire, as was stated in the second chapter of this book. It was, according to the same Prologue, translated by Abraham, Jew and Physician; and once in Castilian, it was also at the Learned King's order, translated into French by Bonaventure of Siena, the King's notary, and was finished in 1264.

Told in the first person, as though Mohammed were actually speaking, the book relates strange and interesting adventures very reminiscent of Dante's great work. Mohammed tells us that he was awakened from sleep by the Angel Gabriel and conveyed on the back of the beast Alborac to the Temple of Jerusalem, there to be greeted by the prophets who had been resurrected from the dead to meet him. After ascending the ladder leading to the First Heaven, he progressed quickly through all of the Seven Heavens of the Ptolemaic system, having been permitted to enter each by Gabriel. The great angel explains to him that he has been chosen as prophet and messenger of God. In each of the Seven Heavens he meets choirs of angels and a prophet. Gabriel leaves him after he has entered the highest heaven, and Mohammed then penetrates veils of glory and at last reaches the very throne of God and speaks with Him. Mohammed has two such meetings with the Deity, after which he descends all the way to the First Heaven to be informed by Gabriel that God has instructed him to guide him and reveal to him all the horrors of hell, which is divided into seven parts. Mohammed passes through them all and observes the torments in each, describes Judgment Day, tells of how souls are weighed in scales, sees the beast representing hell, and traverses the bridge, Azirat, finer than a hair and sharper than a sword, as it passes over the fiery streams of hell. Gabriel is, indeed, Mohammed's guide through the infernal regions. The book ends when Mohammed returns to Mecca to preach his mission. There at last, after many doubts upon the part of the people, he is believed.

Alfonso had known the story no doubt for some time before it was translated at his behest. It had appeared in Rodrigo de Toledo's *Historia Arabum,* "History of the Arabs," and Alfonso had had it incorporated into his *Primera Crónica General.*

I have dwelt upon this strange book because it seems to me that much of Dante's eschatology in his *Divina Commedia* may have stemmed from it or from Moslem sources close to and paralleling it. Controversy over this theory, as laid down by Asín Palacios, a Spanish orientalist, has been heated, but there is much to support it.[20] If Asín Palacios is even partly correct in his ideas, Spain was the channel through which the ideas came to Dante. Asín Palacios made a careful analysis of the *my'ray,* or the ascension into heaven, as it is treated in the works of a Murcian mystic named Ibn 'Arabi (1165–1240), and drew some startling parallels between it and the work of Dante. The general structure of the world beyond the grave, the details and incidents, the punishments, means of travel, etc., in the eastern work and in the Italian are remarkably similar. Those who reject the theory of Asín Palacios object mainly on the grounds that he did not establish any definite contact Dante might have had with the Spanish book. Actually, he did offer good suggestions, and did not confine himself, as these attackers indicate, to the embassy of Bruno Latini, for he mentioned others who traveled from Spain to Italy in Bruno's time. Certainly, whether or not Dante was actually influenced by Spanish translations of Arabic works, such works existed, and the men who might have conveyed these works to Italy traveled between the two countries. And, as has been noted before, Alfonso favored Italian scholars and translators. Indeed, the mention above of Bonaventure of Siena, who translated the book into Old French as *Mohammed's Ladder*, might well have been a point of contact between the two traditions.

"There is no reason," writes Evelyn Proctor, "to reject as impossible, or even improbable, the view that Dante, whose knowledge was encyclopaedic, made use of Arab sources which he knew either through translations or by verbal transmission and such a theory, indeed, solves many difficulties, but to accept that his direct dependence on Moslem thought is as great as Asín Palacios would have us believe is to over-simplify the question." [21]

A great deal of research still will be required before the answer to Asín's assertions can be had. Indeed, more research is needed in all areas of Alfonso's books translated from Arabic. Until such investigations have been carried out, the layman must accept generalities and oversimplifications when he reads about such eastern treatises in medieval Spanish translation.

CHAPTER 9

The Historical Works

I Early Histories in Spain

UNDER the direction and patronage of Alfonso X some of the most remarkable and important of medieval histories came into being. His *Crónica de España*, "Chronicle of Spain," and *Crónica General*, "General Chronicle," are famous even now. Their contribution to the writing of history, not only in method but in materials cited cannot be overlooked, and of even greater value is their contribution to literature. In these great historical documents appear many innovations and new approaches to the very writing of history, but even so, what had been written before, in Spain and abroad, had a strong influence upon the Learned King. Alfonso drew much upon the histories written by his compatriots, all of whom before him had written in Latin rather than the vernacular. The excellence of some of these chronicles is worthy of brief examination since their influence helped to develop what Alfonso undertook. This can be done in a few words, for the Latin histories written in Spain were not plentiful. Indeed, viewed from abroad, these histories may appear to be scant in number as compared to the great body of such works found in England. "It is not only," writes Evelyn Proctor, "that there is nothing to correspond to our thirteenth-century School of St. Albans, there is nothing comparable to the historical works produced in the twelfth century at Worcester, or Malmesbury, or Canterbury, or even the more localized annals at such monasteries as Battle Abbey, Winchester, or Bury St. Edmunds." [1]

Apparently, too, in spite of the nearness of Moorish Spain and the considerable supply of histories written in Arabic, little contact existed before the twelfth century between Islamic and Spanish writers of history. Nor—and this is even more surprising—were there in Spain many records of contemporary events. But as the twelfth century opened, Spaniards began to produce histories worth mentioning, some of which directly influenced the Learned King. Even these suffered by comparison with British historical documents. They are not truly great historical works, but they are important in the development of Spanish history, and some of them even set the patterns followed not only by Alfonso but also in histories subsequent to his times.

The earliest history of any renown at all was the *Liber Chronicorum*, "Book of the Chronicles," of Bishop Pelayo of Oviedo, who treats events no later than 1109. The *Chronica Adelphonsi Imperatoris*, "Chronicle of Alfonso the Emperor," possibly a continuation of the *Liber Chronicorum*, ends in 1147, leaving unchronicled the rest of the reign of Alfonso VII and of his successors until the thirteenth century. Fortunately, more important and complete histories were to follow.

The first of these was the *Historia Silense*, a history written at Silos, which appeared in 1115, the first attempt by a Spaniard to produce authentic history and not mere annals of the rules of various kings. This history did not consider events as late as the end of the twelfth century, but it did deal with the Moors and Arabs in Spain, revealing some knowledge of their histories, and its unknown author made efforts at writing with something like literary style. Evelyn Proctor, an eminent historian in her own right, believes that the author was probably a Mozarab *émigré* from Toledo.[2] In the same century appeared the *Historia Najerense*, a history written at Nájera. It narrates primarily events of ancient times, but toward its conclusion treats historical Spanish events ending in 1109. Probably it was written no earlier than 1160. It is of special importance to Spanish literature, inasmuch as its author made a sudden new departure in historical writing —one to be followed assiduously by later writers, among them the Learned King—in that he utilized poetic sources for the backgrounds of the tenth and eleventh centuries. By poetic sources, of course, is meant the long epic or epic-type poems mentioned in Chapter 3. Later still was the *Historia Roderici*, "History of Roderic," known in literature as Rodrigo or Ruy Díaz de Vivar, the Cid, a figure not even mentioned by Bishop Pelayo. Of the same period was the *Historia Compostelana*, recording the acts of Diego Gelmírez, first Archbishop of Compostela, a book important primarily in ecclesiastical history. These histories and chronicles, plus a few annals, genealogies and saints' lives, are all that have survived from the twelfth century.

But in the thirteenth, the output and quality of history were notable and important. Two of the little-known works and of limited value are the *Gesta Comitum Barcinonensium,* "Deeds of the Counts of Barcelona," the first history of Catalonia, and the *Chronica Latina Regorum Castillae,* "Latin Chronicle of the Kings of Castile." This latter, completed in 1236, treats in a meager way events before 1158, but the reigns of Alfonso VIII (1158–1214) and of his successors are narrated in more detail and appear to be the work of one who was well-informed and writing from personal observation.

The first two truly important and full-scale historical works were written by well-known men, both ecclesiastics. One of these notables was Lucas, Bishop of Tuy, known to the Spaniards as "El Tudense," and the other was Rodrigo Jiménez de Rada, Archbishop of Toledo, referred to as "El Toledano." Lucas wrote his famous *Chronicum Mundi,* "Chronicle of the World," at the behest of Queen Berenguela, grandmother of Alfonso X, about 1236. It is, in part, a universal history of ancient times, but in its latter sections it is national, since it deals with the Visigothic period and with the years of the Reconquest, both of which it treats in considerable detail, especially as concerns Castile and León.

Archbishop Rodrigo wrote the best of the early histories, surpassing even Lucas of Tuy. He had traveled to Paris and even to Rome and had read foreign histories, observing much about their makeup and preparation. No less a personage than Ferdinand III commissioned him to write his great *De Rebus Hispaniae,* "On the Affairs of Spain," if the Prologue of this work can be trusted. The Archbishop believed, as did most Spaniards before him, including St. Isidore of Seville, that the Spanish people were descended directly from the Visigoths, a fact which led them to belittle their Roman heritage. One reads in his works of the legendary populating of Spain by the sons of Japhet, and of the exploits of Hercules, a hero still dear to Spaniards and still considered by them to be an early inhabitant of their land. There are, too, more historical accounts of the wanderings of the Goths before they entered Spain, of their kingdom in the Peninsula, of the Moorish invasion and of the Reconquest, with special attention given to the deeds of the rulers of Asturias, León, and Castile, although those of Navarre and Aragon are not completely omitted. More important was the fact that Archbishop Rodrigo consulted the histories of the Spanish Arabs so as to present accounts pertinent to an understanding of the wars and political and cultural contacts between Spanish Christendom and Spanish Islam. His sources for the period of the Reconquest were the then known histories and to some extent the epic poems, but these latter he drew upon with care and with good critical judgment.

The latter part of the *De Rebus Hispaniae* is more reliable than the earlier parts, and more lengthy, too, principally because in it the author deals with events closer to his own times and in some cases with those he must have observed, because the last two books are based upon his own experiences and upon contemporary official documents. His other two histories—both of which deal with events that touch Spain—are valuable documents. The *Historia Romanorum,* "History of the Romans," treats primarily the period of Roman history in which Spain was involved, for example, the times of the Punic Wars, and the wars between Caesar and Pompey; his *Historia Arabum,* "History of the Arabs," starts with Mohammed and narrates the events in the lives of those leaders who followed him before the conquest of Spain. After this, it traces the history of Islam in the West, and particularly in Spain, up until the twelfth century. Arabic sources were used almost exclusively in its composition.

History in Spain, then, at least in the first half of the thirteenth century, had been written with care by men of wisdom and learning. The time was ripe, therefore, when Alfonso X embarked upon the two vast historical projects which helped to make him famous.

II *Alfonsine Histories: The* Primera Crónica General

Alfonso was not content to continue the writing of history in the old way. He became an innovator and thereby was far ahead of the historians of the century, whether Spanish or foreign. Gonzalo Menéndez Pidal best states this in his discussion, "Alfonso X, el Sabio," in Guillermo Díaz-Plaja's *Historia General de las Literaturas Hispánicas*. I translate as follows: "Against the particularistic character which the medieval chronicle had, the Learned King undertook a national history, and this with a very Catholic spirit, which will cause the *Crónica General de España* to be not the chronicle of one event nor of one kingdom, but of a nation which did not have an existence politically, but which already existed in the Alfonsine mind with firm reality. This concept was not absolutely new: the Latin history of don Rodrigo Jiménez de Rada was already a work which embraced the entirety of the new peninsular kingdoms in a concept of totality, and with this the Toledan did nothing short of showing himself to be consistent with the political concept of a new and young Castilian realm." [3]

Alfonso showed an interest hitherto unknown in all phases of history. He did not let his historians spend all their energies upon important events alone—battles, political crises, and the succession of rulers, for example; in addition to these matters he insisted upon the treatment of cultural and social life and thereby produced a history, not of certain classes, but of all classes of Spanish society. To accomplish such a detailed coverage of the history of Spain and even of the world, he assembled all available historical documents, including classic Latin writings, as well as medieval and Spanish authors who wrote in Latin, and Arabic and Moorish histories, some written in Spain and some abroad. And because he was no doubt influenced by the techniques of "El Toledano" in the use of literary sources, he too continued to borrow consistently from the same or similar materials.

It would be well here to view briefly the general nature of the two great Alfonsine histories before studying either in detail. The first was the history of Spain, variously known as the *Primera Crónica General* and as the *Crónica General de España,* which latter title is more descriptive of the actual content. But since Menéndez Pidal insisted upon the former title, it will continue to be used. This great Spanish scholar published a text of the *Primera Crónica General* based upon two Escorial manuscripts, one of which deals with Spanish history up to the Moorish conquest, the other covering the events from the period of Pelayo to the death of Ferdinand III in 1252.[4]

1. Sources

The sources of the *Primera Crónica General* were many. Fortunately it is not difficult to trace most of these. Among the principal Latin histories used in its preparation were the following: Suetonius' *Lives of the Caesars;* the *Heroides* of Ovid, a work more closely associated with literature than history; the *Pharsalia* of Lucan, likewise of literary vintage. The most important historians from the Gothic period were Orosius, St. Isidore of Seville, and Jordanus. Medieval works which deeply influenced the Alfonsine were the *Speculum Historiale,* "Mirror of History," of Vincent of Beauvais, and in particular the aforementioned histories of "El Tudense" and "El Toledano." Nor did the Learned King fail to take cognizance of Byzantine chronicles, or fail to utilize to the fullest extent both Christian and Arabic histories and, more important, the epic poetry of Spain, whether the material for these came from earlier histories or directly from the poems themselves.

A reliable staff of historians and other specialists was always available. And translators were on hand to render works from different languages. Furthermore, the King, and the historians he employed, abbreviated, expanded, edited, and otherwise reworked the books used as primary materials. Naturally, historians must have borne the heaviest responsibility, and the names of some have come down to us: Jofré de Loaysa, Juan Gil de Zamora, Martín de Córdoba, and Bernardo de Brihuega.

To return to the use of sources, one can point to the *De Rebus Hispaniae* of Archbishop Rodrigo, cited previously. His history served as a kind of framework into which Alfonso's historians inserted parts of the Archbishop's *Historia Arabum* and *Historia Romanorum,* thereby bringing universal history and Spanish history together. Evelyn Proctor[5] effectively demonstrates how these insertions were made, using as an example the treatment of the life of Mohammed taken from the *Historia Arabum,* which the historians interpolated in almost literal translation, skilfully weaving it into the history of the Visigoths which they drew from the *De Rebus Hispaniae.* She believes that this, and the parts of Arabic history drawn from Lucas of Tuy's *Chronicum Mundi,* provided the Arabic background and that the King and his historians did not go directly to the Arabic sources themselves. Indeed, it would be unwise to say that these chroniclers of Alfonso always used even Lucas de Tuy or Rodrigo Jiménez de Rada in their Latin versions, for both had been rendered into the vernacular. It is demonstrable that at least in part these historians were consulted in vernacular translation.

Apparently in the *Primera Crónica General* the reign of Ferdinand III is almost a verbatim translation from *De Rebus Hispaniae*. And sometimes two accounts of the same events occur, apparently from two different sources with no attempt to verify which is the more accurate. Again, there are sequences in the *Primera Crónica General* which cannot be definitely traced as to source.

Of greatest interest to students of literature are the uses of the epic sources already alluded to, but now to be treated in more detail. Begun in the earlier chronicles and perpetuated in the works of Lucas of Tuy and Archbishop Rodrigo, this technique was used extensively in the Alfonsine chronicles. The *Primera Crónica General* drew upon the lost epics *Bernardo del Carpio*, the *Siete Infantes de Lara, Sancho el Fuerte,* and the *Cid.* Even where the Alfonsine work translates from the *De Rebus Hispaniae*, passages are added, based apparently upon poetic sources. The *Peregrinación del Rey de Francia,* for example, is translated from the Latin of Rodrigo de Toledo, but from the lost poem itself are added interesting details which the Archbishop seems to have regarded as too unhistorical to be included in his work. On the other hand, the historians employed by Alfonso, and the King himself as he edited the work, rejected this view and included much more from the poetic epics. Perhaps they felt, as modern scholars do, that such epics as the *Poema de Mío Cid* contained much truly historical material. But apparently, also, they accepted certain facts that modern investigation has proved to be fictitious, and by so doing Alfonso's scholars served literature more faithfully than history. So devoted were these historians to the epic sources that they went far beyond paraphrasing, and at times even inserted entire epic sequences into their accounts. This can be demonstrated by studying some of these lines and proving that they are written in the epic meter of the *mester de juglaría,* but set down in paragraphs as though they were prose.

The *Primera Crónica General,* then, has preserved an entire repertory of some of the lost epics and even certain verbatim parts of these epics. Without this great Alfonsine history a good deal of epic material would not have survived, and we owe to the *Primera Crónica General* many facts that can be found nowhere else. Without this history we would know much less, for example, about daily life, the law courts before standard laws were written, about marriages and feuds, indeed, about a whole corpus of materials that made up the social history of Spain.

This dedication to literary sources may have led the Alfonsine historians to devote a disproportionate amount of space to some characters, whereas in other cases too little space was given. The most notable example of the former is the case of the Cid. In the *Primera Crónica General* one can read the entire life and actions of the great Castilian warrior while, to illustrate a case of too little space, one finds only meager accounts of the life of King Alfonso VI, the Cid's contemporary and liege lord. This attention to the Cid is not entirely the fault of the Alfonsine historians, although they may indeed have preferred to write about so compelling a hero as Rodrigo Díaz de Bivar. Part of the blame may lie with earlier historians who were scant in their treatment of the king and disproportionate in their attention to the warrior. Besides, there was one Latin chronicle, it will be recalled, the *Historia Roderici,* devoted entirely to the Cid, and this was a book much used by the Alfonsine historians. Lastly, Arabic chronicles narrated events in which the Cid was involved, and these Arabic sources, directly or indirectly, touched the writing of the *Primera Crónica General.*

2. *Influence of Alfonsine History*

The importance of Alfonsine history to students of literature is great indeed. It reveals the vast amount of classical, oriental, and European literature known in those times; it points to whole areas of medieval Spanish literature now lost in the mists of time, and it preserves in prosification all that we have of the lost epics. As regards its contribution to history, in spite of its proclivity toward inclusion of nonhistorical facts, its reputation is also bright. The *Primera Crónica General* was the first historical work of any importance written in Spanish. From it evolved all Spanish histories and, since it served these, not only as a mine of source material but also as a model of style and presentation, and since it made a new departure in historical writing through the inclusion of literary documents not ordinarily seen by historians, it is invaluable. What a pity that the events treated are no later than the death of Ferdinand III, Alfonso's father, and that nothing is recounted of the Learned King himself or of his times which would have been well-known to the men who composed the *Crónica*.

Menéndez Pidal has stated that the *Primera Crónica General* was begun about 1270 and that the part of the great work which deals with the Moslem Conquest of Spain was actually not written in Alfonso's time at all, but in the reign of his son, Sancho IV. Evelyn Proctor, on the other hand, thinks that the entire book, even the second part devoted to Moslem affairs in Spain, was written in the time of Alfonso X. If Sancho's patronage was actually responsible for the parts indicated by Menéndez Pidal, Sancho did no more than recast a redaction prepared by the Alfonsine historians. Evelyn Proctor's place among European historians, her professional preparation as a historian, and her research—all of which belongs to the realm of history—would seem to give greater weight to her deductions than to Menéndez Pidal's in this case.[6]

Space will not permit a long discussion here of the influence of the *Primera Crónica General* upon later Spanish histories. Let it suffice to say that all subsequent histories leaned heavily upon this great Alfonsine document. To begin with, large parts of it were soon translated into Portuguese, Galician, Catalan, and Aragonese; men like Don Juan Manuel, the King's famous nephew, wrote recensions of it which were briefer, less specialized, and intended to present an account of Spanish history to the public in general; histories like the *Crónica de 1344* appeared, which gave résumés of the content of the *Primera Crónica General* and then added brief accounts of events which occurred after it had been written; still others, after careful editing, substituted for the material drawn from old epics, new poetic materials taken from the poems of contemporary troubadours and even from the Spanish ballads, demonstrating even as they changed the content, that they preferred to perpetuate the old technique of literary borrowing—all of which is patent in the *Crónica de 1404* and the *Crónica de Juan II*. Gonzalo Menéndez Pidal points out that even Arabic historians made use of the *Primera Crónica General,* for he cites the Islamic history of Jatib de Loja (1372–1424) who inserted into his work a summary of the Christian kings of the Reconquest taken from the Alfonsine work.[7]

3. Style

The style of the *Primera Crónica General* illustrates the verbosity, and at the same time, the detail and picturesque literary quality of the prose developed at the Learned King's court. One finds a great deal of explanatory material, a definite attempt to tell the reader that what is cited at a given place in the history has been introduced before, and perhaps even discussed before and explained. Such prose contains vivid passages not easily forgotten, and the commentary accompanying historical fact and evidence is obviously the result of careful thought and planning. Parts of the work read like a novel, a fact that should not be regarded as strange, when one considers that certain sequences of the *Primera Crónica* were drawn from literary sources, and that epic poems rendered into prosification partake not only of the quality, but partially of the form of the novel. The following example, taken from the great Alfonsine history treats, as though they were true, of the legendary deeds of Hercules in Spain. To the historians the Greek demi-god was an actual person living in historical times. The almost literal translation I have made from Chapter Six will illustrate the mingling of fact and fancy as well as the general tone and style of this kind of material in the *Primera Crónica:*

OF HOW HERCULES FOUGHT WITH KING GERION AND SLEW HIM

"Hercules, of whom you have already heard previously, as soon as he had constructed those two images of Cadiz and Seville, had the desire to see all the land that was called Hesperia, and he set out along the coast of the sea until he reached a place where the city of Lisbon now is, and this was populated after Troy had been destroyed the second time; and a grandson of Ulysses, who had the same name, began to people it, and because he did not see the end of this before his death, he commanded a daughter of his named Bona to finish it, and she did so and joined together the name of her father and her own, and gave it the name Lixbona [Lisbon]. And when Hercules came to that place, he knew that a very powerful king was in Hesperia who held the land from the Tagus to the Duero, and because he had seven provinces under his authority it was related in the ancient fables that he had seven heads; and this was Gerion, and he was such a very strong and swift giant, that by his strength he had conquered the land, and men had perforce to give him half of all they had, their sons and daughters and their possessions, and those who did not wish to do so were killed by him. And for this he was much hated by all the people, but they did not dare to oppose him since they had no one who could defend them; and when they learned that Hercules was coming, they sent to say to him that he, who had done so many good deeds and had taken so many men from under oppression and evil rule, might come to their aid, and that they would give him the entire land. When Hercules heard this, he was much pleased and he went there quickly; for even though he was of the lineage of the giants and very strong, he was not a wild man nor of bad governance, but was rather very pious to good men and very harsh and strong toward evil men, and when he heard the complaints of those people, he grieved for them and he went to them. And when Gerion learned this, he went with his armies to that place at which later the city called Crunna was established, which was then a wilderness. Hercules sent to tell Gerion that the people did not deserve to be killed nor to suffer, but that they [Hercules and Gerion] should fight hand to hand; and that whichever one of them conquered should have all the land. And Gerion was bold in his own valor, and since he was the larger, he agreed. And they struggled for three days and were not able to overcome one another; and at last Hercules won and cut off his head. And he ordered built in that place a great tower, and commanded that the head of Gerion be placed in the foundation, and had a great city established, causing to be written down the names of the men and the women who came to populate it, and the first inhabitant who came was a woman named Crunna,[8] and therefore he gave the name to the city."

After treating events more truly historical, such as the conquest of Spain by the Romans, the historians touched upon more recent matters. The following passage from Chapter 564 narrates something of the beginning of the Reconquest:

OF HOW PRINCE DON PELAYO ROSE UP IN THE ASTURIAS

"Four years of the rule of Prince Don Pelayo having passed, which was in the Era of 755, when the Christian Era was in its year 717, and the fourth in the Era of Leo, with all Spain in sorrow and beaten down by the many evils and misfortunes which had come upon her just as we have mentioned, God, omnipotent in all things, even though He was angry at her, did not desire to forget His mercy, and He remembered her grace, and He wished therefore to protect the Prince Don Pelayo with His countenance like a tiny spark from which later will spring up a fire in the land. Thus Don Pelayo fled before Wittiza[9] when he tried to blind him, just as we stated before this, although he had been his shield bearer and carried his sword for him; and he took refuge in Cantabria and sheltered himself there. And when he learned that the Christians had been defeated and that all their chivalry was lost, he took a sister whom he had and went with her to the Asturias to see if in the vastness of the mountains he might keep alive some gleam of light near which Christians might assemble, for the Moors had now conquered all the rest of Spain, just as we have said; and they broke the power of the Goths so that there was no one there who might defend them, save some few who established themselves likewise in the Asturias and in Biscay and in Alava and in Guizpuzcoa, because the mountains are very high, and in the Rucones Mountains and in Aragon. And these God wished to protect so that the light of Christianity and his servants might not be extinguished in all Spain. The Moors placed their governors in each town to gather tribute from the farmers who remained in the lands of vines and trees which they had not wished to destroy. . . . In this year Lothar, King of France, died, and after him, Charles I ruled for twenty years."

The scope of the *Primera Crónica General* is so vast that the reader today is appalled by it. In referring to this work I cite the definitive edition of Ramón Menéndez Pidal, who has divided it into two parts:[10] Part I begins with a chapter entitled OF HOW MOSES WROTE THE BOOK WHOSE TITLE IS GENESIS, AND OF THE FLOOD, and ends with Chapter 565 which bears the title OF HOW MUNUCA MARRIED THE SISTER OF THE PRINCE DON PELAYO AGAINST HIS WILL, AND OF HOW HE TOOK HER AWAY FROM HIM AFTERWARDS AND SENT KNIGHTS TO TARIFA TO IMPRISON HIM. The time span of the first part, then, covers the centuries from Moses to the eighth-century Count Pelayo. The chapters vary considerably in length, some requiring several large modern printed pages, whereas others run to less than twenty lines. The narration of events moved rapidly, for by the time the historians had reached Chapter 16 one reads of the Phoenician entry into and conquest of Spain, and by Chapter 21 the Punic Wars have begun. The presentation is not always chronological, because the historians seem to have believed that it was necessary to give background for given events, after the events had been discussed. Thus, in the midst of the discussion of the Punic Wars (264–146 B.C.) they describe the life of Dido, Queen of Carthage, who lived some thousand years earlier and was contemporary with the Trojan War. So taken, by the way, were they by the accounts of Dido's life, found in the *Aeneid* and in Roman histories, that they even gave space to such details as the letter she wrote to Aeneas.

The history of Rome is, of course, treated with greatest attention, inasmuch as sources for it were plentiful and in Latin, a language read by all European scholars. Chapter 112 offers a list of the Roman consuls and "other princes" of Rome, beginning with Brutus Lucius Junius, the first of the consuls, and ending with Julius Caesar's consulship. For numerous chapters thereafter we read of the life and deeds of Julius, of his character and even of such minor matters as his poetic abilities, his habits, and his friendships. The list of Roman emperors follows, complete in Chapter 121. Rather long accounts follow of the lives of Augustus, Tiberius, and all the other Roman emperors. Caligula's physical description, taken from the *Lives of the Caesars*, deserves to be translated here, so as to give the reader an idea of the minutiae of detail included by the Alfonsine historians. The translation is a part of Chapter 165. After giving the earlier life of Caligula, when he was well-mannered and moderate, the later events and later characteristics of the emperor appear as follows:

"And know that Gaius [Caligula] was a man of large body and he was ugly, and his neck and legs were thin, and his jaws and his eyes sunken, and his forehead, broad and curved; he had sparse hair and on the top of the head none, and what he had was always erect. And therefore when he passed, no one dared to look at him from behind, nor to mention the word goat in any way, lest he die because of it. And his face was frightening by nature, and he made it even more so by art, for he would gaze into his mirror and try to set it in frightful grimaces. . . . He did not walk in Rome dressed in the manner of a man, nor shod like one; for he wore vestments brightly hued, all covered with precious stones and his fingers covered with rings, and his wrists with bracelets of gold; and he used to go so before all the people; at other times garbed in the robes of a woman. . . ."

III *The* General Estoria

The Learned King and his collaborators had written, probably by 1272, some four hundred chapters of the *Primera Crónica General* when the second great historical project was begun which was to be, in the minds of the writers, a complete history of the world. It never reached this status, since the last events it treats were those in the life of St. Anne, mother of the Blessed Virgin. For this reason, of course, the *General Estoria* lacks completeness, omitting the rise of Christianity and its influence upon universal events, and of course, the development of the history of the West after the days of Augustus. The great history is divided into six parts, not all of which even now have been edited, perhaps owing to its very vastness. Even in the unfinished form the *General Estoria* is four times as long as the *Primera Crónica General*. Had the historians been able to finish it according to the proportions envisaged, it would be the longest history in the world.

For the beginnings, as has been mentioned, the historians utilized Holy Scripture—the Pentateuch up to New Testament accounts of St. Anne, mother of the Blessed Virgin. The Vulgate was the version used as the primary source for these materials, but even Hebrew texts are cited. The history of Egypt, drawn to some extent from Biblical accounts, received a new treatment in the annals of the West, for to the Biblical accounts was added the history of Egypt as seen by the Moslem chroniclers. Of course the works of Josephus, Peter Comestor, and all the then known historians of the Jews and the other important empires of the Ancient World were studied and their works drawn upon. Classical writers and even Greek and Roman mythology were important sources, and the Christian historians of Alfonso managed to include the immortal gods in their accounts, considering them not as deities, but as great kings and queens and other rulers, who by their repute and power, came to be regarded as gods by their subjects. In this way Alfonso was able to reconcile the myth of Antiquity with the Christian belief. In this he followed, of course, the apologetics of both Christian and Jewish scholars of previous centuries.

The history of the Orient, not well-known to Alfonsine historians, save through the Greeks and Romans, was nevertheless to find a place in the *General Estoria*. Legend and history both treated the conquest of India by Alexander, and indeed, as was mentioned in Chapter 3, Spaniards had already rendered into their vernacular the *Book of Alexander*, which was a very encyclopedia of lore, much of it eastern. And of course Greek and Roman historians had dealt with the great Macedonian's entry into India and with his wars there with the Hindu king, Porus.

It will be of value to read in translation some selections taken from the areas of universal history already discussed. In Book VII, Chapter XXXV we read of King Jupiter and come to understand the Alfonsine historians' conception of the gods of Antiquity.

"In this city of Athens King Jupiter was born, and there he studied and learned, and to so great an extent that he understood very well the entire *Trivium* and *Quadrivium*, which are the Seven Liberal Arts, due to the reasons which we have recounted to you earlier, and they are set in order among themselves according to their nature in this way: the first is Grammar; the second, Dialectic; the third, Rhetoric; the fourth, Arithmetic; the fifth, Music; the sixth, Geometry; the seventh, Astronomy. . . ." The history then continues for two whole chapters a detailed explanation of these Seven Liberal Arts, and in Chapter XXXVII explains how the Greeks discovered Music:

"The Greeks began, before other men, to familiarize themselves with and to travel over the sea a great deal; and some of them strove mightily to be able to enter into it so as to prove whether they might find the boundaries of the parts beyond it. And they traveled so much that they came to a place where they heard sounds and voices which seemed to them to be sweeter and more delightful than anything could be, and they began to discuss it among themselves. . . ."

They landed, according to the history, and saw a mountain crag, and thinking that the sounds emanating from it were the voices of sirens, they approached. But at this juncture a great wind blew them into the sea, killing many. The survivors returned home, made up a new band of explorers and approached the crag from another direction, so as to escape the perilous wind. They observed the mountain with great care, as the next passage explains:

"And standing there, they looked carefully at the crag and saw how it was hollowed out inside, and that there were in it seven apertures made in gradation of size, some wide, others more narrow, and some high and others low, and they were made from one size to another. And they saw how the winds entered into the waters of the sea and came out through those holes and made those exceedingly sweet sounds.

"And there they learned the art of Music and found the seven mutations of its scale. And because they learned it from the wind and the waves, they gave it the name *moys*, for this word *moys* has in the language of the Greeks the meaning of 'water' in the language of Castile. . . ."

One can read of Prometheus the Giant in Book IX, Chapter XLV as the following brief passage will clearly illustrate: "With fifty-two years of the reign of Joseph passed, according as Jerome relates, as well as Eusebius and others, Prometheus, son of Japhet, son of Titan the Giant, was a very wise man and he formed some images of clay in the shape of men in such a way that by his skill and knowledge he made them move and travel by their own power. And others tell that this Prometheus by his powers flew up in the air, and that through his science he carried torches in his hand and reached the sun, and kindled the torches in the rays of the sun and then descended; and with these infusions into those images of clay, they took life from it and went about on their own power."

Then to explain all this to the Christian reader, the historians continue: "But so that this will not seem a fable to the good and wise, Eusebius and Jerome treat it, as do other sages who speak of it, and they say that this story means that so wise was this Prometheus that he imparted knowledge skilfully to mankind in such a way that he made of fools, and those without any knowledge until their deaths, wise and learned men to such an extent that he took them from the death of ignorance and placed them in the life of knowledge. And from this *exemplum* and explanation comes the fable. . . ."

No brief treatment could possibly even so much as touch upon the copious materials found in the *Crónica General,* but even so I feel that a few further examples of passages from the great book can best help to bring it into focus for the modern reader. A translation of it is a desideratum, but one is not likely to be forthcoming, given the length of this book. Of Alexander's march toward India we read:

"Alexander the Great, as soon as he had taken possession of the lands of which you have heard in the chapter preceding this one, moved from there with his host and entered into a desert place, cold and dark, and the men, even though they were close together, could scarcely see and recognize one another. And they rode through that dark land for seven days, and at the end of the seventh day they came to a river which had hot waters, and on the other side of it they found very beautiful women who dwelt there and who wore garments exceedingly bizarre, and they rode horses and carried weapons of gold because they had not iron or copper out of which to make them, nor was there a single male among them all. . . .

"And Alexander wished to pass beyond the river to them, but in no way could he for it was wide and filled with dragons and other huge wild beasts. . . ."

After long travels Alexander approached the borders of India:

"And going on farther, Alexander and his army came to the outermost jungles of India; and Alexander rested there on the bank of a river which they call Buemar. And about the eleventh hour a great multitude of elephants began to emerge from the jungle, and they marched against his army. Then Alexander mounted his horse and began to ride against the elephants and ordered the Macedonians to mount and follow him against the elephants; and the elephants heard the noise of Alexander and his knights who were coming and they stretched out their trunks, huge things with which they pick things up, and extended them to seize them. And when the Macedonians saw the elephants in such guise, they were very much terrified and for no reason did they dare to go to them. When Alexander saw this he said to them: 'Strong knights, do not turn back, for we can overcome the elephants!' And he had swine brought up and made to grunt where they could frighten the elephants, for the thing in the world that elephants fear most and are terrified by are the gruntings of swine. And so it was done, and when the elephants heard the grunting of the pigs, and the sounds of the trumpets, they began to take fright. And Alexander and his knights followed them, and as they caught up with them they struck them down with spears and swords and slew many of them, and they carried off from them their teeth and horns and returned to the host."

Although it is true that the Alfonsine historians did not arrange all their materials chronologically and did not hesitate to use fictitious and legendary accounts and events in no way historical, nevertheless they did not work without plan and form based upon considerable critical and well-planned correlation. In this they at least approximate modern historiography and removed themselves from the medieval patterns they might have followed. In so far as was possible, they attempted to follow historical chronology and erred only when they were unable to develop such chronology.

The influence of this great history was much felt by later writers, as was natural. Leomarte used it as the background for his *Sumas de Historia,* "Summary of History," and the author of the *Cronica Troyana,* "Trojan Chronicle," mentioned in an earlier chapter, found it invaluable. And "El Tostado" utilized it when he composed his *Comentarios a la Crítica de Eusebius,* "Commentaries to the Criticism of Eusebius." Menéndez Pidal says in his aforementioned essay, ". . . the fact that it did not treat the periods which were most important, Christianity and the new European nationalities, caused it to lose much of the fame which it should have received because of its original conception." [11]

The two great Alfonsine histories, the *Primera Crónica General* or *Crónica de España* and the *Crónica General*, sometimes referred to as the *Gran e General Estoria* or *Historia Universal*, may be regarded by us among the greatest contributions of the Learned King to European culture. Spanish literature would be much less rich but for these histories, and our knowledge of medieval man's understanding of the universe, of the past and of his own times, would be much less complete than it is. Lastly, the style developed in these works matches anything in all the Alfonsine repertory and did much to develop subsequent writing.

CHAPTER 10

Summation

THE "Thirteenth-Century Renaissance" inaugurated by Alfonso X, el Sabio, brought to his native land unique and excellent innovations in many areas of knowledge. His treatment of oriental fiction, exemplified in *Calila e Digna,* opened to the readers of Spain and of Spanish a hitherto unknown fictional world, new literary motifs and a kind of didacticism, or pseudodidacticism long present in the East, but not in the Spanish language before his time. His faith and devotion to the Blessed Virgin and his desire to make her many miracles known to his people, his eagerness to honor her not only in verse but also in music and in pictorial art, gave his subjects the marvelous *Cantigas de Santa María.* In its pages lies a wealth of knowledge as yet hardly touched; in its musical notation musicologists know is to be found one of the keys to a modern understanding of medieval melody. In its miniatures is to be found a considerable part of the development of thirteenth-century painting. The Learned King's *Cantigas Profanas,* not the equal of the more famous *Cantigas de Santa María,* nevertheless have a value all their own, for they reveal a side of Alfonso's character not otherwise identifiable and they link the poetry of the Learned King and his court with the courtly currents of European verse.

Actually Alfonso X was more renowned for his nonliterary works, although even these for the most part belong to literature. His famous scientific books, so closely linked with medieval belief and superstition—the *Libros de Astronomía* and the *Lapidarios,* actually influenced belles-lettres, but at the same time served the history of the sciences and introduced much of eastern scientific lore into the West. The King's historical projects—the great *Estoria General* and the *Primera Crónica General*—were far more than historical documents, although as such they made remarkable contributions and were as copious and multisourced as any medieval histories. Their second contribution is to the very history of Spanish literature, since they drew so heavily upon the epics and epico-narrative poetry of the Spanish people, inserting whole sequences of these poems in prosified form, into the sections dealing with Spanish history. In this way Alfonsine history preserved the material of the lost epics which otherwise would not have survived the ages.

Famous also and far-reaching were the legalistic works of Alfonso. His great code of laws, the *Siete Partidas,* which made its way with Spanish conquerors and settlers to the farthermost corners of the New World, into Africa and even into the Philippines, has continued to survive, and of course is even today the foundation of law in the mother land and in her present possessions. No body of writing in the Spanish Middle Ages is more revelatory of daily life, of custom and of medieval Spanish thinking than this great book, for it overlooks no area of man's obligation to his God, to his state, and to his fellow men.

If the life and political and military events of the Learned King have not been well remembered, his contributions to the arts and letters, to the sciences, to historiography, to the law, and to music make him live on more actively in the minds of his people than many of the kings whose conquests and political triumphs have been forgotten.

The grand stairway up which one climbs to reach the portico and doorways of the Biblioteca Nacional in Madrid is occupied by the statue of only one personage. It is not the figure of Cervantes, as one might have suspected, nor of Columbus, nor of Isabella, nor of some Spanish saint. The statue is that of the Learned King, seated on his throne. I feel that nothing is more fitting than that the monarch who founded what we can consider rightly to have been the first national library of the Spanish people should be so honored.

Notes and References

Chapter One

1. Many histories of Spain can be consulted for the backgrounds of the Spanish people. A concise, but very valuable and authoritative, one is William C. Atkinson, *A History of Spain and Portugal* (London, 1960). For the student who needs a general study no book is better. The best of the longer histories is that of Antonio Ballesteros y Beretta, *Historia de España y su Influencia en la Historia Universal* (Barcelona, 1943–48) in twelve volumes. Roman, Visigothic, and Moorish Spain all receive long treatment.

2. See the excellent history of R. Altamira, *A History of Spain* (New York, 1949) which is the best manual of Spanish history in one volume. The *Diccionario de Historia de España* (Madrid, 1952) in two volumes offers some 3,000 pages of useful information.

3. The history of the Moors in Spain may be profitably consulted in A. González Palencia, *Historia de la España Musulmana* (Madrid, 1945) and his *Moros y Cristianos en la España Medieval* (Madrid, 1945). The authoritative study of E. Levi-Provençal, *Histoire de l'Espagne Musulmane* (Paris, 1950–53) is the best of all.

Chapter Two

1. The only definitive history of the life and reign of Alfonso X is that of Antonio Ballesteros y Beretta, *Alfonso X el Sabio* (Barcelona, 1963). In its 1,142 pages, followed by a series of instructive and beautiful illustrations, resides perhaps all that is known about this king. The short but informative book for young people by Juan Ríos Sarmiento, *La Vida y los Libros de Alfonso el Sabio* (Barcelona, 1943) offers a succinct but helpful account of the king's reign and his works.

2. Ballesteros, 48.

3. Ballesteros, 50–51.

4. Ríos Sarmiento, 11–21.

5. Ballesteros, 60. The translation is mine.

6. Ríos Sarmiento, 160–61. The translation is mine.

Chapter Three

1. Ernst Robert Curtius, in *European Literature and the Latin Middle Ages* (New York, 1948), has a long and complete treatise on the Latin writings in the Middle Ages and their ties with the classical period.

2. Helen Waddell, *The Wandering Scholars* (New York, 1955) treats of the Latin songs of the wandering troubadours, and much of what she states is applicable to Spain.

3. Américo Castro's *The Structure of Spanish History* (Princeton, N. J., 1954), pp. 130–70, is one of the most provocative studies in existence on the influence of the pilgrims who journeyed to Compostela. See also Georgiana G. King, *The Way of St. James* (New York, 1920).

4. J. Th. Welter, *L'Exemplum dans la Littérature Religieuse et Didactique du Moyen Âge* (Paris, 1914); Thomas F. Crane, *The Exempla of Jacques de Vitry* (London, 1890); Léopold Hervieux, *Les Fabulistes Latins* (Paris, 1896); and the Introduction to John E. Keller, *The Book of the Wiles of Women* (Chapel Hill, N. C., 1956), give sound treatment of the medieval *exempla*.

5. Students interested in general surveys of medieval Spanish literature should consult A. Millares Carlo, *Historia de la Literatura Española hasta Fines del Siglo XV* (Mexico, 1950); Guillermo Díaz-Plaja, *Historia General de las Literaturas Hispánicas* (Barcelona, 1949) Vol. I; or one of the many written in English, such as George T. Northup, *An Introduction to Spanish Literature* (Chicago, 1960) or Richard Chandler and Kessel Schwartz, *A New History of Spanish Literature* (Baton Rouge, La., 1961).

6. Gerald Brenan, *The Literature of the Spanish People* (New York, 1957), pp. 17–35 and 466–70, offers a lucid treatment of these early lyrics.

7. See note 5 for Chapter 6 for the complete bibliographical data for these collections of songs.

8. R. Menéndez Pidal, "Razón de amor, con los Denuestos del Agua y el Vino," *Revue Hispanique*, XIII (1905), 602–18.

9. The definitive edition of this work is in Ramón Menéndez Pidal, *Cantar de Mío Cid. Texto, Gramática, y Vocabulario* in his *Obras Completas* (Madrid, 1944–45). The best translation is that of Leslie B. Simpson, *The Poem of the Cid* (Los Angeles, 1957).

10. The best study of the epic cycles is that of Manuel Milá y Fontanals, *De la Poesía Heroico-Popular Castellana* (Barcelona, 1959).

11. See the edition of R. Foulché-Delbosc, "*Vida de Santa Maria Egipciaqua*," (Barcelona: Textos Castellanos Antiguos, 1907), or that of Archer M. Huntington, *Libro de los Tres Reyes de Oriente* (New York, 1904).

12. The best edition is that of J. C. Marden, *Poema de Fernán González* (Baltimore, 1904).

13. See the definitive edition of Raymond S. Willis, *Libro de Alexandre* (Paris, 1934).

14. See Raymond Grismer and Elizabeth Atkins, *El Libro de Apolonio*, (Minneapolis, 1936).

15. See Antonio G. Solalinde, *Milagros de Nuestra Señora* (Madrid, 1922).

16. Ballesteros y Beretta, *Alfonso X el Sabio*, 123–25.

17. See the edition of Pedro José Pidal, "Disputa del Alma y el Cuerpo," *Diario Español* (June 22, 1856), 2–3; see the edition of Ramón Menéndez Pidal, "Elena y María," *Revista de Filología Española* I (1914), 52–96; and the edition of F. Morel-Fatio, "Razón de Amor con los Denuestos del agua y el vino," *Textes Castillanes Inedits du XII° Siècle* in *Romania* XVI (1887), 368–79.

18. See the introduction to the edition of R. Menéndez Pidal, "Auto de los Reyes Magos," *Revista de Archivos, Bibliotecas y Museos* IV (1900), 453–62.

19. The best edition of the first is by Hermann Knust, *Flores de Filosofía*, published in *Dos Obras Didácticas* (Madrid, 1878); for the second see Knust's "Poridad de Poridades," *Jahrbuch für Romanische und Englische Literatur* X (1869); the best edition of the *Bonium*, so named from the philosopher who is its protagonist, is that of H. Knust, and "Bocados de Oro," in *Mittheitungen aus dem Eskurial* (Tubingen, 1879).

20. The Book of *Calila e Digna* is the subject of the entire Chapter 2 of our present book. References will be found there, of course, to texts, editions, studies, etc.

21. See the edition of John E. Keller (Chapel Hill, N. C., 1953) and the second and enlarged edition, 1959; see Keller's translation of the book with the title *The Book of the Wiles of Women* (Chapel Hill, 1956).

22. The best edition to date is that of F. Lauchert, *Historia del Rey Anemur e de Barlaam e de Josaphat, Romanische Forschungen*, VII (1893), 33–402.

Chapter Four

1. John E. Keller discusses this matter thoroughly in the Prologue of the edition prepared by him and Robert W. Linker, *Calila e Digna* (Madrid, 1966).

2. J. E. Keller, *The Book of the Wiles of Women*, p. 15.

3. See the edition of Agapito Rey, *Castigos e Documentos para Bien Vivir* (Bloomington, Indiana, 1952).

[176]

Notes and References

4. The edition of H. Knust, *Juan Manuel, El Libro de los Exiemplos del Conde Lucanor* (Leipzig, 1900) is still the best.

5. For the best bibliographical data for the Arabic *Kalila wa-Dimna* see Victor Chauvin, *Bibliographie des Ouvrages Arabes ou Relatifs aux Arabes.* Tome II. *Kalilah* (Liege, 1897).

6. See the *Encyclopedia of Islam* (Leyden and London, 1913), p. 122.

7. *Don Quixote,* translation of Peter Motteux (New York, 1930), p. 464.

8. The best edition of the *Panchatantra* is that of Theodore Benfey, *Pantschantra: Fünf Bücher indischer Fablen, Märchen, und Erzählungen* (Leipzig, 1859). An excellent and delightful translation is that of Arthur Ryder, *The Panchatantra* (Chicago, 1958).

9. All detailed discussion of the book *Calila e Digna* is based upon the edition of John E. Keller and Robert W. Linker, mentioned in note 1.

Chapter Five

1. I have treated in some detail the rivalry between the shrines of the Virgin Mary and the famous Tomb of Saint James at Compostela in "King Alfonso's Virgin of Villa-Sirga, Rival of St. James of Compostela," *Middle Ages-Reformation-Volkskunde, Festschrift for John G. Kunstmann* (Chapel Hill, N. C., 1959), pp. 75–81.

2. All quotations from the *Cantigas de Santa María* are taken from the new and definitive edition of Walter Mettmann listed in the Bibliography.

3. Professor Evelyn Proctor of St. Hugh's College, Oxford, discusses the dating of the manuscripts in her excellent book entitled *Alfonso X of Castile, Patron of Literature and Learning* (Oxford, 1951), pp. 44–46.

4. Proctor, pp. 37–38.

5. Mettmann, pp. vii–xxiv, gives an extremely detailed paleographical description of the four codices of the *Cantigas de Santa María.*

6. Leopoldo A. de Cueto, Marqués de Valmar, *Cantigas de Santa María* (Madrid, 1889).

7. Martín de Riquer, *Historia de la Literatura Universal,* I (Barcelona, 1957), p. 326.

8. Chapter 6, which treats of Alfonso's poetry exclusive of the *Cantigas de Santa María,* gives more detailed information about this variety of poetry.

9. See Frank Calcott, *The Supernatural in Early Spanish Literature* (New York, 1923); A. F. G. Bell, " 'Las Cantigas de Santa María' of Alfonso X," *Modern Language Notes* X (1915), 338–48. For Mussafia's

classification consult the Introduction to the edition of the *Cantigas* of the Marqués de Valmar; Angel Valbuena Prat, *Historia de la Literatura Española*. I (Barcelona, 1946), 124–28.

10. *Crónicas de los Reyes de Castilla* I (Madrid, 1953), ed. by Cayetano Rosell, and published as Vol. 66 of the *Biblioteca de Autores Españoles*.

11. Marqués de Valmar, Introduction.

12. The most helpful of my articles on this matter is "Folklore in the *Cantigas* of Alfonso el Sabio," *Southern Folklore Quarterly* XXIII (1959), 175–83.

13. John E. Keller, "Daily Living as Presented in the *Canticles* of Alfonso the Learned," *Speculum* XXXIII (1958), 484–89; and the same author's "Daily Living as Revealed in Alfonso's *Cantigas*," *Kentucky Foreign Language Quarterly* VII (1960), 207–10.

14. Américo Castro, *The Structure of Spanish History* (Princeton, N. J., 1954), pp. 361–68.

15. Dorothy Clotelle Clarke, "Versification in Alfonso el Sabio's *Cantigas*," *Hispanic Review* XXIII (1955), 83–98.

16. See Gerald Brenan, *The Literature of the Spanish People* (New York, 1957), pp. 63–68; 466–70.

17. Gilbert Chase, *The Music of Spain* (New York, 1941), p. 24.

18. I translate here from R. Menéndez Pidal, "Las Cantigas del Rey Sabio," *La Ilustración Española y Americana* XXXIX (1895), 163.

19. Gilbert Chase, p. 26.

20. Julián Ribera, *La Música de las Cantigas* (Madrid, 1922).

21. Higinio Anglés, *La Música de las Cantigas de Santa María del Rey Alfonso el Sabio* (Barcelona, 1943), p. 11.

22. Anglés, p. 11.

23. *Ibid.*

24. Anglés, p. 12.

25. Two excellent phonographic recordings have been made recently: *Las Cantigas de Santa María del Rey Alfonso el Sabio*, produced by Experiences Anonymes in *Music of the Middle Ages*, Vol. III—The Thirteenth Century with Russell Oberlin, Countertenor and Joseph Iadone, Lutist; and *Spanish Medieval Music: Twelve Cantigas de Santa María, Liturgy of Santiago de Compostela, Mass in Honor of the Blessed Virgin* produced by Pro Música.

26. Charles L. Nelson, "Literary and Pictorial Treatment of the Devil in the *Cantigas de Santa María*." (Unpublished Master's thesis, University of North Carolina, 1964), pp. 45–47.

27. José Guerrero Lovillo, *Las Cantigas, Estudio Arqueológico de sus Miniaturas* (Madrid, 1949) reproduces all the miniatures of the Escorial Codex, but not, alas, in color. Still, even in black-and-white

reproduction one can see a surprising amount of detail and gain at least some idea of the remarkable richness of this Alfonsine book.

28. Guerrero Lovillo, pp. 34–35.
29. Guerrero Lovillo, pp. 22–23.
30. J. E. Keller, "Daily Living as Presented in the *Canticles* of Alfonso the Learned," *Speculum* XXXIII (1958), 488.
31. Guerrero Lovillo, p. 19, quotes these lines from the King's will.

Chapter Six

1. Francisco López Estrada's *Introducción a la Literatura Medieval Española* (Madrid, 1962), 2nd ed., enlarged, pp. 130–43, is designed for students and offers a concise but valuable treatment; see also J. Filguera Valverde, "Lírica Medieval Gallega y Portuguesa," *Historia General de las Literaturas Hispánicas*, I (Barcelona, 1949), pp. 543–642, for an intensive and detailed study. Gerald Brenan, *The Literature of the Spanish People* (New York, 1957), pp. 51–68, offers a brief but singularly lucid and informative study. George T. Northup, *An Introduction to Spanish Literature*, 3rd ed., revised and enlarged by Nicholson B. Adams (Chicago, 1960), pp. 97–102, is general, but good for orientation.

2. Gerald Brenan, p. 58.
3. The poem is number 70 in the *Cancioneiro Portuguez da Vaticana*, ed. by Theophilo Braga (Lisbon, 1878), p. 14.
4. Gerald Brenan, p. 59.
5. The editions used for this chapter are the following (Any reference to these texts will point, therefore, to the editions here cited). *Cancioneiro Portugues da Vaticana*, ed. of Theophilo Braga (Lisbon: Imprenta Nacional, 1900); *Cancioneiro da Biblioteca Nacional Antiguo Colocci-Brancuti, Leitura, Comentários e Glossário* (Lisbon, 1949–58); and *Cancioneiro da Ajuda*, ed. by Carolina Michaëlis (Halle, 1904).
6. Cesare de Lollis, "Cantigas de Amor e de Maldezir di Alfonso el Sabio, Rei di Castiglia," *Studi di Filologia Romanza*, II(1887), 31–66.
7. Martín de Riquer, *Historia de la Literatura Universal*, I (Barcelona, 1957), p. 327.
8. *Afonso X, o Sábio, Cantigas de Santa Maria*, I, ed. of Walter Mettmann (Lisbon, 1959), p. 117.
9. James Fitzmaurice-Kelly, *The Oxford Book of Spanish Verse* (Oxford, 1942), p. 8.

Chapter Seven

1. Fortunately the vast *Siete Partidas* has been translated into English by an American legist. All translations from this book, save the

first which will be seen in note 3, come from Samuel Parsons Scott, *Las Siete Partidas* (New York, 1931).

2. I have translated the word *rayen*, from the verb *raer*, "to scrape," as "they erased," because parchments were scraped to remove what had been written, and this means of erasure would lack meaning to the modern reader.

3. This passage of the *Siete Partidas* comes from British Museum Add. MS. 20787, fol. Ir, col. 2. The translation is my own.

4. Evelyn S. Proctor, *Alfonso X of Castile, Patron of Literature and Learning* (Oxford, 1951), p. 49.

5. *Ibid.*, p. 71.

6. Samuel Astley Dunham, *History of Spain and Portugal* (London, 1833–42), Vol. VI, 131–32.

7. *Dictionnaire Historique* (Paris, 1810), Vol. I, 257.

8. See the section entitled "Spain" by Rafael Altamira in *A General Survey of Events, Sources, Persons and Movements in Continental Legal History* (Boston, 1912), p. 654.

9. M. Rico y Sinobas, *Los Libros del Saber de Astronomía* (Madrid, 1863–67) VII, p. 135.

10. *General Estoria*, I, 3.b. The translation is my own.

11. R. Altamira, 629. The translation is my own.

12. *Ibid.* The translation is my own.

13. *Ibid.* The translation is my own.

14. *Ibid.*, 634. The translation is my own.

15. Scott, liii–iv.

16. *Ibid.*, lix.

Chapter Eight

1. See the edition of Manuel Rico y Sinobas, *Los Libros del Saber de Astronomía* (Madrid, 1863–67), the best edition; an interesting study, also, is J. L. E. Dreyer, "On the Original Form of the Alfonsine Tables," *Monthly Notices of the Royal Astronomical Society* LXXX (1920), 243–67.

2. Ballesteros y Beretta, *Historia de España . . .* (Barcelona, 1943–48), 245–46.

3. Since the *Tablas Alfonsinas* have never had previous translation to English, I have translated the passages used in this chapter.

4. Evelyn S. Proctor, *Alfonso X of Castile, Patron of Literature and Learning* (Oxford, 1951), p. 10.

5. *Ibid.*

6. It has been reproduced in facsimile with a Prologue by José Fernández Montaña by Imprenta La Iberia, (Madrid, 1881), with full color which is remarkable for this date of printing.

7. Proctor, p. 12.

8. The *Era Española*, based on the era of Julius Caesar, lasted until well into the fourteenth century in both Castile and Aragon. In order to compute the Christian Era, our own, from the Era Española, one subtracts 38 years from the latter.

9. John E. Keller, "The Lapidary of the Learned King," *Gems and Gemology* (Winter, 1957–58), 105–10; 118–21. All translations are taken from this article.

10. Keller, "The Lapidary of the Learned King," p. 118.

11. *Ibid.*, 118.

12. *Ibid.*

13. *Ibid.*, 119.

14. *Ibid.*

15. *Ibid.*

16. *Ibid.*, 120.

17. *Ibid.*

18. Proctor, p. 12.

19. Since no translation has been made heretofore of the *Libro de Ajedrez, Dados y Tablas*, all the translations of passages are my own.

20. M. Asín Palacios, *La Escatología Musulmana en la Divina Comedia* (Madrid, 1943).

21. Proctor, p. 21.

Chapter Nine

1. Evelyn S. Proctor, *Alfonso X of Castile, Patron of Literature and Learning* (Oxford, 1951), p. 78.

2. *Ibid.*, p. 77.

3. Guillermo Díaz-Plaja, *Historia General de las Literaturas Hispánicas* (Barcelona, 1949), Vol. I, 437.

4. Proctor, pp. 85–96, gives a good discussion of this.

5. *Ibid.*, 96–97.

6. *Ibid.*, 86 ff.

7. Díaz-Plaja, I, 441.

8. La Coruña is the name of the city today.

9. Wittiza, a Visigothic king who died in 710, after he had been replaced by Rodrigo, last of the Visigothic rulers.

10. Ramón Menéndez Pidal, *Primera Crónica General de España* (Madrid, 1955), two vols.

11. Díaz-Plaja, I, 442.

Selected Bibliography

PRIMARY SOURCES

1. Books by Alfonso or Written under His Patronage

Calila e Digna. Critical edition by John E. Keller and Robert W. Linker (Madrid: Consejo Superior de Investigaciones Científicas, 1966). This edition presents both surviving manuscripts and in a long introduction studies the sources, influences, and content of eastern and western versions.

Cantigas de Santa María. Walter Mettmann, ed. (Coimbra: Acta Universitatis Conimbrigensis, 1959–64). Three volumes. This, the definitive edition, offers the most up-to-date study on the *Cantigas.*

Cantigas Profanas: The best editions are the following:

Cancioneiro da Ajuda. Carolina Michäelis de Vasconcellos, ed. (Halle: Niemeyer, 1904).

Cancioneiro da Biblioteca Nacional (*Antiguo Colocci-Brancuti*). Elza Pacheco Machado and José Pedro Machado, eds. (Lisbon: 1949–1958.

Cancioneiro Portuguez da Vaticana. Theophilo Braga, ed. (Lisbon: Imprenta Nacional, 1900).

Crónica General o Sea Historia de España que Mandó Componer Alfonso el Sabio y se Continuaba bajo Sancho IV en 1289. Ramón Menéndez Pidal, ed. (Madrid: Bailly-Balliere, 1906). This is found in Vol. V of *Nueva Biblioteca de Autores Españoles.* Re-edited by him with the collaboration of A. G. Solalinde, Manuel Muños Cortés, and José Gómez Pérez (Madrid: Editorial Gredos, 1955).

Fuero Real. Marcelo Martínez Alcubilla, ed., in *Códigos Antiguos de España* (Madrid: López Camacho, 1885).

General Estoria. Primera Parte. Antonio G. Solalinde, ed. (Madrid: Molina, 1930). *Segunda Parte,* Solalinde, Lloyd A. Kasten, and Victor R. B. Oelschläger, eds. (Madrid: Consejo Superior de Investigaciones Científicas, 1957).

Selected Bibliography

Lapidario, Reproducción Fotolitográfica. Prologue by José Fernández Montaña (Madrid: La Iberia, 1881). Excellent color facsimile.

Libro de Ajedrez. Das Spanische Schachzabelbuch des Königs Alfons des Weisen von Jahr 1283. Prologue by John G. White (Leipzig: Karl W. Hiersemann, 1913). Excellent facsimile in black and white.

Libro del Saber de Astronomía. Manuel Rico y Sinobas, ed. (Madrid: E. Aguado, 1863–67). Five vols.

Libro de las Cruces. Lloyd A. Kasten and Lawrence B. Kiddle, eds. (Madrid: Consejo Superior de Investigaciones Científicas, 1961).

SECONDARY SOURCES

1. Doctoral Dissertations and Masters' Theses

Elise F. Dexter. "Sources of the *Cantigas* of Alfonso el Sabio" (diss. Wisconsin, 1926).

Charles L. Nelson. "Elements of Humor in Medieval Spanish *Exempla*" (diss. North Carolina, 1965). Studies the major collections of *exempla*, but the section on *Calila e Digna* is most pertinent to Alfonso X.

————. "Literary and Pictorial Treatment of the Devil in the *Cantigas de Santa María*" (thesis, North Carolina, 1964). Gives a detailed treatment of artistic techniques in the *Cantigas*.

John H. Nunemaker. "Index of Stones in the Lapidary of Alfonso X with Identification in Other Lapidaries" (diss., Wisconsin, 1928). Helpful because it covers points not covered elsewhere.

Theodore H. Shoemaker. "Alfonso X as Historian" (diss., Wisconsin, 1941). A valuable supplement to Alfonsine historiography.

2. Books

Altamira, Rafael. *A History of Spain* (New York: Macmillan, 1918).

Anglés, Higinio P. *La Música de las Cantigas de Santa María del Rey Alfonso el Sabio. Facsímil, Transcripción y Estudio Crítico* (Barcelona: Diputación Provincial de Barcelona: Biblioteca Central, 1943). This monumental study opens up new vistas and new approaches to the study of medieval musical transcription.

Atkinson, William C. *A History of Spain and Portugal* (London: Whitefriars Press, 1960). An excellent short history by a professor familiar with Spanish literature.

Ballesteros y Baretta, Antonio. *Alfonso el Sabio* (Barcelona: Salvat Editores, 1963). This 1,142-page book is the definitive study of the life of the Learned King. Some small part of it is a treatment of his literary and scientific works.

Brenan, Gerald. *The Literature of the Spanish People* (New York: Meridian Books, 1957). Readable, sound, up to date. One of the very best general treatments of medieval Spanish letters, and especially good for poetry.

Castro, Américo. *The Structure of Spanish History* (Princeton: Princeton University Press, 1954). Provocative commentary. A controversial study of many aspects of Spanish literature by one of the great scholars.

Chandler, Richard E. and Kessel Schwartz. *A New History of Spanish Literature* (Baton Rouge: University of Louisiana Press, 1961). A very useful and reliable book. Literature is treated by genre rather than by chronological approaches.

Chase, Gilbert. *The Music of Spain* (New York: W. W. Norton, 1941). The treatment of Alfonsine and medieval music is brief, but sound.

Cueto, Leopoldo A. *Cantigas de Santa María de Alfonso el Sabio* (Madrid: Real Academia Española, 1889). Copious notes, good introduction, indispensable for background.

Curtius, Ernst R. *European Literature and the Latin Middle Ages* (New York: Pantheon Books, 1948). An excellent English translation from German of this important book. Curtius's is the most useful study of the unbroken tradition of Latin literature in the Middle Ages which was so influential upon medieval literatures.

Denomy, Alexander J. *The Heresy of Courtly Love* (New York: McMullen, 1947). The most up-to-date and best general study in English.

Díaz-Plaja, Guillermo. *Historia General de las Literaturas Hispánicas* (Barcelona: Editorial Barna, 1951). This great work is a series of studies by experts in the many genres discussed, brought together and edited by Díaz-Plaja. Invaluable for concise and reliable discussions.

Fisher, John H. *The Medieval Literature of Western Europe, A Review of Research, Mainly 1930–1960* (New York: The New York University Press, and London: University of London Press, 1966). This book gives in Chapter 8 and in Chapter 10 comprehensive bibliographies of Spanish and Portuguese medieval literatures.

González Palencia, A. *Historia de la España Musulmana* (Barcelona: Editorial Labor, 1945). Concise, but authoritative and useful.

———. *Moros y Cristianos en la España Medieval* (Barcelona: Editorial Labor, 1945). A very good treatment of the two cultures.

Green, Otis H. *Spain and the Western Tradition* (Madison: University of Wisconsin Press, 1963). Masterly treatment of many aspects of Spanish literature. Vols. I, II, and III have been published.

Guerrero Lovillo, José. *Las Cantigas. Estudio Arqueológico de sus*

Miniaturas (Madrid: Consejo Superior de Investigaciones Científicas, 1949). Unsurpassed in detail and replete with excellent sketches and black-and-white reproductions of the miniatures.

Holmes, Urban T. *History of Old French Literature* (New York: F. S. Crofts, 1937). The best and only complete history of Old French literature in English. Very fine bibliographies.

Las Siete Partidas, trans. Samuel Parsons Scott (New York: Commerce Clearing House, Inc., 1931). A monumental piece of scholarship which makes this Alfonsine work available to English readers. Excellent introduction and background of law.

Menéndez y Pelayo, Marcelino. *Orígenes de la Novela* (Buenos Aires: Espasa Calpe, 1946). These three volumes offer one of the most complete studies of the rise and development of Spanish fiction.

Milá y Fontanals, Manuel. *De la Poesía Heroica-Popular Castellana* (Madrid: Consejo Superior de Investigaciones Científicas, 1959). This recent translation of the French original is updated. Invaluable for an understanding of medieval lyrics.

Millares Carlo, Agustín. *Historia de la Literatura Española hasta Fines del Siglo* XV (México: Antiguo Librería Robredo, 1950). This is the best general history of Old Spanish literature with chapters followed by excellent bibliographies.

Northup, George T. Revised by Nicholson B. Adams. *An Introduction to Spanish Literature* (Chicago: University of Chicago Press, 1960). A useful, standard, and valuable work. One of the most up to date of such studies.

Proctor, Evelyn S. *Alfonso X of Castile, Patron of Literature and Learning* (Oxford: Clarendon Press, 1951). An excellent treatment of Alfonso X from the viewpoint of an eminent historian.

Riquer, Martín de. *Historia de la Literatura Universal* (Barcelona: Editorial Noguer, 1957). Concise in its treatment of individual works, this three-volume book is nonetheless valuable and filled with good criticism and stimulating ideas.

Sarmiento, Juan Ríos. *La Vida y los Libros de Alfonso el Sabio* (Barcelona: Editorial Juventud, 1943). This modest book for students in Spain contains valuable information and is attractively presented.

Solalinde, A. G. *Antología de Alfonso el Sabio* (Buenos Aires: Colección Austral, 1940). Brief selections with adequate introductory remarks for each.

Waddell, Helen. *The Wandering Scholars* (New York: Doubleday, 1955). This study of the Goliards and of the Latin poetry of the Middle Ages is sound and very readable. Excellent renditions of the Latin verse in English.

3. Periodical Articles

Asín Palacios, Miguel. "El Juicio del P. Mariana sobre Alfonso el Sabio," *Al-Andalus*, VII (1942), 479. Gives valuable critical appraisal of Alfonso by one of Spain's great modern scholars.

Bohigas Balaguer, Pedro. "La Visión de Alfonso X y las Profecías de Merlin," *Revista de Filología Española*, XXV (1941), 383–98. Connects Alfonso X with the non-Hispanic materials of Merlin's prophecies.

Castro, Américo. "Acerca del Castellano Escrito en Torno a Alfonso el Sabio," *Filologia Romanza* I, Fasc. 4 (1954), 1–11. Shows the quality and style of Alfonsine prose as found in the greatest Alfonsine manuscripts.

Cerulli, Enrico. "Il Libro della Scala e la Questione delle Fonti Arabospagnuole della *Divina Commedia*," *Studi e Testi*, 150 [of the Vatican], (1949), 574. Attempts to analyze and explain the reasons for believing that Hispano-Arabic texts influenced Dante.

Clarke, Dorothy Clotelle. "Versification in Alfonso el Sabio's *Cantigas*," *Hispanic Review*, XXIII (1955), 83–98. A complete treatment of all the verse forms in the *Cantigas*.

Domínguez Bordona, Jesús. "*El Libro de los Juicios de las Estrellas*, traducido para Alfonso el Sabio," *Revista de la Biblioteca, Archivos y Museo del Ayuntamiento de Madrid*, VIII (1931), 171–76. A brief but scholarly note.

Fitzmaurice-Kelly, James. "Some Early Spanish Historians," *Transactions of the Royal Historical Society*, I, 3rd Series (1907), 139–56. Includes Alfonso's histories as well as some treatment of those histories before his times.

Johnson, Mildred E. "*Las Siete Partidas* as a University Catalogue," *Hispania*, XXXVI (1951), 91–93. A brief note on the curriculum mentioned by Alfonso in the *Partidas*.

Keller, John E. "Daily Living as Presented in the *Canticles* of Alfonso the Learned," *Speculum*, XXXIII (1958), 484–89. Treats of various aspects of rural and urban life and offers two illustrations in black and white from Alfonsine minatures in the *Cantigas*.

———, "Folklore in the *Cantigas* of Alfonso el Sabio," *Southern Folklore Quarterly*, XXIII (1959), 175–83. Using some twenty-odd of the *Cantigas*, this article treats most of the major classes of folklore to be found in these songs.

———, "The Lapidary of the Learned King," *Gems and Gemology*, (Winter 1957–58), 105–10 and 118–21. Translates several of the chapters in the *Lapidaries* and explains the importance of this Alfonsine work.

Lollis, Cesare de. "Cantigas de Amor e de Maldezir di Alfonso el Sabio, Rei di Castiglia," *Studi di Filologia Romanza*, II (1887), 31–66. Successfully proves by internal evidence that the Alfonso of León and Castile mentioned as an author in the *Cantigas Profanas* is Alfonso X and no other Alfonso.

London, Gardiner. "Bibliografía de Estudios sobre la Vida y Obra de Alfonso X el Sabio," *Boletín de Filología Española*, II (1960), 18–31. The most complete bibliography, but even so, lacking in many items.

Menéndez Pidal, Gonzalo. "Como Trabajaron las Escuelas Alfonsíes," *Nueva Revista de Filología Hispánica*, V (1951), 363–80. A fine explication of Alfonsine collaborators based upon the testimony of primary sources.

Millás Villacrosa, José. "El Literalismo de los Traductores de la Corte de Alfonso el Sabio," *Al-Andalus*, I (1933), 155–87. A detailed description and study about the style and techniques of Alfonso's translators.

Proctor, Evelyn S. "Materials for the Reign of Alfonso X of Castile, 1252–1284," *Oxford Essays in Medieval History Presented to Herbert Edward Salter* (Oxford, 1934), 104–21. A masterly brief study of these matters by one of England's greatest modern historians.

Rey, Agapito. "Correspondence of the Spanish Miracles of the Virgin," *Romanic Review*, XIX (1928), 151–53. Explains the correspondence of miracles in the *Cantigas*, the *Milagros* of Berceo and certain other collections of miracles of the Virgin.

Ruiz y Ruiz, Lina A. "Gonzalo de Berceo y Alfonso X el Sabio: los *Milagros de Nuestra Señora* y las *Cantigas*," *Universidad de San Carlos*, XXIV (1951), 22–90. A lengthy comparative study of the content of the two works.

Solalinde, A. G. See the long list of articles, studies, and anthologies of this scholar in Gardiner London's *Bibliografía* mentioned above.

Steiger, Arnald. "Alfonso X, el Sabio y la Idea Imperial," *Arbor*, VI (1946), 389–482. Studies in great detail Alfonso's attempts to gain the title of Emperor of the Holy Roman Empire, showing the legality of Alfonso's claims.

Trend, John B. "Alfonso el Sabio and the Game of Chess," *Revue Hispanique*, LXXI (1933), 393–403. A brief study of the techniques and importance of Alfonso's famous book on chess.

Urrestarazu, Sinesio. "*Las Cantigas* de Alfonso X el Sabio: una Modificación a la Historia de la Música," *Revista de las Indias,* XVII (1943), 221–60. New and valuable remarks on the influence of Alfonso's *Cantigas.*

Van Scoy, Herbert. "Alfonso X as a Lexicographer," *Hispanic Review,* VIII (1940), 227–84. Valuable and informative remarks about Alfonsine vocabulary and the breadth of Alfonsine lexicography.

Index

Abdallah ben Almuqaffa, 46, 51, 52, 54, 55, 56, 57, 60
Aben Quich, 141–2
Abenragel, 147
Aben-Yuzaf, 36–7
Abolays, 141–2
Abulafia, Samuel ha-Levi, 136
Acts 20: 9–12, 75
adab, 54, 58
Adam, 94
Aeneas, 165
Aeneid, 165
Aesop, 49
Aesop's Fables, 55
Affonso, Rei de Castella, 101
Africa, 22, 24, 25, 26, 28, 33, 37, 117, 122, 173
Ajuda, 100
Alarcón, 114
Alarcos, 26, 28
Álava, 164
Albans, St. School of, 158
al-Battani, 146
Alborac, 150
Alcántara, 22
Alcuzum, Sea of, 143
Alexander, Era of, 138
Alexander the Great, 42, 46, 138, 167, 169, 170
Alexander IV, Pope, 34
Alfaquín de Toledo, Abraham, 136
Alfonsine Era, 138
Alfonsine Tables, 32
Alfonso of Aragon, 33
Alfonso of Portugal, 34, 36
Alfonso "el Niño," 32
Alfonso, Pedro, 122
Alfonso VI, 134, 160
Alfonso VII, 135, 154

Alfonso VIII, 26, 30, 153
Alfonso XI, 120
Alfred of Sareschel, 136
Algarbe, 34
Ali, 28
Ali, son of Alschah Faresi, 56
Ali Iben Abi-l-Rijal, 146–7
Alice in Wonderland, 55
Almohades, 28, 39
Almorávides, 27, 28, 39
Altamira, Rafael, 117, 119, 120, 121
Alvandexaver, Sultan of Egypt, 74
al-Zarqali, 32, 137
amadigo, 99
Amores (of Ovid), 106
Andalusia, 25, 26, 28, 29, 35, 80
Anglés, Higinio, 85, 86
Anne, St., 166
Apolonius of Tyre, 42
Arabian Nights, 47, 55, 62
Arabs, 39, 152, 154, 156
Aragon, 21, 26, 29, 33, 36, 39, 98, 156, 164
Aragonese, 40, 70, 122
arte mayor, 82
Arthurian Cycle, 50
Asia, 117, 122
assonance, 41
Assumption of the Virgin, 45
astrology, 141, 146, 147
astronomy, 141, 146, 147
Asturians, 25, 164
Asturias, 24, 27, 112, 156
Atlantic Ocean, 122
Atlas Mountains, 28
Augustine, St., 121
Augustus, 165, 166
Auto de los Reyes Magos, 45
Ávila, 114

Index

Index

Index